JAGUAR XK-E

1961-75

JAGUAR XK-E

1961-75

A Documentation by Walter Zeichner

1469 Morstein Road, West Chester, Pennsylvania 19380

This volume of the Schiffer Automotive Series contains the history of a classic car as seen in its advertisements—the Jaguar XK-E—a sports car that sells today for more than twice its original price. The accurate facsimile reproductions of the catalogs and brochures from the Sixties and early Seventies, affords an interesting look back to the "youthful years" of the XK-E. The documentation is completed by tables of all technical details and press comments.

For his support in assembling the materials, we thank Kai Jacobson, whose collection has so often contributed to completing our SAS documentations.

Halwart Schrader
Editor

Translated from the German by Dr. Edward Force,
Central Connecticut State University.

Printed in the United States of America.
ISBN: 0-88740-247-X

This book originally published under the title,
Jaguar E-Type 1961-75,
by Schrader Automobil Bücher,
Handels-GmbH, München.
© 1988. ISBN: 3-922617-42-5.

Published by Schiffer Publishing, Ltd.
1469 Morstein Road
West Chester, Pennsylvania 19380
Please write for a free catalog.
This book may be purchased from the publisher.
Please include $2.00 postage.
Try your bookstore first.

Contents

The English Way of Life: XK-E Fascination

What automobiles with the brand name of Jaguar have to offer the fan and connoisseur cannot be expressed in dry technical descriptions. And it is not superb technology alone that makes the Jaguar fascinating—it is rather an aura that has grown historically and, not least, has come to embody a good bit of the so-called English way of life.

Only a few cars have ever offered such brilliant performance, aesthetics in design and exclusiveness at a price that is anything but exaggerated. The XK-E in particular was worth every penny. This sports car was a milestone in the history of the Jaguar firm, as well as the culmination of a series that had begun before the war with the famous SS 100. This roadster and its descendants, the XK 120, 140 and 150, rank among the most popular classics of British auto building.

Yet the development of the XK-E did not depend on the traditional XK 150 of the 1950s. It was a new design, and yet it was simultaneously, so to speak, an everyday version of the D-Type competition car, with many of that car's outstanding design characteristics. The backbone of the Jaguar XK-E was a monocoque-type cell of great rigidity, welded together from profiled sheet steel, to the rear end of which a subframe was attached for the rear axle and its independently sprung wheels. Also, at the front of the XK-E there was a subframe to carry the six-cylinder motor, and the motor hood was hinged at the very front and opened, as a part of the body, all the way back to the windshield—the motor and front axle were just as accessible as those of the D-Type competition car.

At the Geneva Salon in the spring of 1961, the public greeted the appearance of the XK-E with enthusiasm. With this car, Jaguar had fulfilled the wishes of countless enthusiasts who wanted a full-blooded sports car again, and had observed with anxiety the increasing comfortable nature of certain models to suit the high demands of American customers.

But even those who had no conception of the competition-type construction of the XK-E could only be fascinated by the good looks of its bodywork, which was also quite reminiscent of the D-Type. The red coupe that was tastefully introduced that spring attracted admiration with its sleek lines, that express power and dynamism like scarcely any other car even today, but without any of the "muscle-car" effect of, for example, the Chevrolet Corvette.

The front half of the XK-E, as it stood on its sparkling chrome spoked wheels, consisted of practically nothing but the gently curving motor hood with the visible bulge in the middle and the louvers at the sides. The plexiglas-covered headlights that did not disturb the smooth body lines were particularly striking, as was the characteristic radiator grille with its side bumpers.

With this uncompromising two-seater, Sir William Lyons and his designer, Malcolm Sayer, had returned to the sports-car philosophy that had been introduced in its purest form after the war by the XK 120. The roof section too, as well as the luggage area that curved softly to the end of the body, blended perfectly with the coupe's charming appearance; the car's side panels curved outward noticeably, making the XK-E appear to have a narrow track. Slightly antiquated sportiness of typically British style prevailed inside, with big Smiths instruments to show the road and engine speeds, plus an integrated clock and a large wooden steering wheel with pierced spokes. In this model Jaguar refrained from its otherwise lavish use of hardwood; instead, the central part of the instrument panel consisted of

Left: One of the famous ancestors of the XK-E: The Jaguar XK 120 Roadster of 1949—here in an early version with lightweight aluminum body. The car generated great enthusiasm from the start.

Below: Jaguar XK 150, built from 1957 to 1961—the direct ancestor of the XK-E. The 3.4-liter six-cylinder motor meanwhile had 190 DIN HP, the tuned S version had over 250.

an aluminum plate, on which four small gauges and the light switch were mounted above six small switches, the lighter, the ignition lock and the starter button. All of this provided a purposeful, functional atmosphere, yet not without charm. The bucket seats provided for a comfortable ride, as long as the driver had not grown too tall. Generous window areas, with the rather steep windshield serviced by three wipers, made the cockpit airy and provided a good view.

When one released the motor hood—in the first car this was still done by means of a special key—an imposing view was offered the beholder. The well-known 3.8-liter straight six-cylinder motor of the XK 150 was an old-style long-stroke engine that offered

7

268 HP and legendary elasticity. To be sure, the motor could not stand high engine speeds very well, but they were scarcely necessary, for the dohc motor developed great power just barely over idling speed. Expressed in figures, this meant a top speed of circa 240 kph and acceleration from zero to 100 kph in just under seven seconds.

But the way this motor unleashed its power was much more impressive than mere numbers. Apparently effortlessly, quite unlike Italian and German high-performance motors that all too easily gave one a nervous feeling, the XK-E put itself into motion steadily. A fifth gear could be dispensed with easily, from 20 kph on, in direct fourth gear one had almost full power on the clutch. This can scarcely be achieved any more with the current small-displacement motors made to run at high speeds, but in the XK-E it scarcely made a difference at all whether one wanted to accelerate from 20 to 50 or from 120 to 150 kph in fourth gear. For either operation the car took less than six seconds, only from about 160 kph on did the air resistance become noticeable to the passengers, who until then had been pushed forward evenly in their seats.

The power brake system, with conventionally located front brakes and rear disc brakes working on the differential, was sufficient to handle this power in the XK-E, unlike the similarly powerful XK 120 and 140, which had often had brake trouble.

The only bitter taste in this thoroughly fascinating car was left by the gearbox, in which first gear was still unsynchronized and did not exactly stand out in terms of easy use and freedom from maintenance. The pedal distance of the otherwise soft clutch was also much too great, and many missed the overdrive of the XK models, so advantageous at high speeds, as there was no room for its mechanism in the XK-E.

Besides the coupe, one could also get a roadster with a flat trunk lid that suited the proportions of the XK-E just as superbly. It added to the absolutely unmistakable appearance of the Jaguar, that few cars before or since have equaled. In the roadster, especially with the top up (there was also a fiberglass hardtop), there was naturally a little less space than in the coupe, but on the other hand it was a special pleasure to drive such a powerful car with the top down.

The XK-E was designed as an uncompromising two-seater, and so there was not much space for luggage under the roadster's trunk lid. since most of the space there was taken up by the fuel tank and spare wheel. The situation was somewhat better in the coupe, whose luggage space could be loaded conveniently via the lid that opened from the side, and the trunk lids of the coupe and roadster had to be released from inside the car by using a lever behind the driver's seat. Unfortunately, the otherwise very useful big rear window of the coupe also gave a panoramic view of all the luggage inside.

A car with such breathtaking performance, sold at such a reasonable price, might have been a dangerous toy in the hands of many customers unfamiliar with such high-performance sports cars if the makers had not made sure that the car was easy to control. The XK-E 3.8 liter at first pushed itself outward at the front on fast turns, but could easily be brought back on course via the gas pedal, and sporting drifts could be performed without any great risk. Thus one could practically steer the car through a curve with the gas pedal. It was inadvisable, though, to come off the gas on fast curves, since the rear end came around fast and the car was not easy to control then.

So the XK-E was predestined for long fast trips, for the suspension also had almost sedanlike character-

Upper left: The Jaguar D-Type racing sports car. From 1954 to 1956 it ranked among the "greats" in international competition. Above: The C-Type in action in 1952.

Left: This was the XK-SS. Only sixteen of these full-blooded cars were built in 1956-57. It was meant to be the street version of the D-Type and suggested the lines of the later XK-E . . .

istics, and the passengers were kindly spared any excessively loud suspension or motor noise. This car combined pleasant performance and the purebred sports-car style of earlier days with the well-developed comfort of the Sixties, thus amounting to one of the most alluring automotive offers of its time.

The Jaguar XK-E was built in this firm for about three years. Of the roughly 15,500 cars produced in these years, barely 3000 had right-hand drive and stayed home in Britain; the great majority took the trip across the Atlantic. During these years, which brought no significant changes in the original design, an improved model was developed and finally introduced in October of 1964. A cylinder bore increased by 5.07 mm raised the displacement of the veteran motor to 4.2 liters, which resulted in practically no improvement in performance, but it raised the maximum torque, so that a stronger crankshaft was built to take the heavier load. The bores were grouped so that the old cylinder head could be retained.

A welcome addition was a fully synchronized gearbox that could be shifted much more easily and sportingly, thus freeing the XK-E from its one serious fault. Seen from outside, there was no difference between the 3.8 and the 4.2 liter XK-E's, but things had changed inside. The aluminum in the center of the dashboard and on the central console had given way to a black leather covering, blending with the other furnishings; there was now a glove compartment between the seats, and the coupe's luggage space was now more luxurious. Naturally, all this brought a slight increase in weight, which scarcely influenced the performance. Another popular change was the use of polyurethane parts, which allowed the service interval for the steering

and front wheel joints to be lengthened from 5000 to 12,000 miles.

Drivers taller than 180cm still had trouble finding enough room when in the driver's seat, but this situation had been improved by better seat backs and longer seat rails angled backward.

In March of 1966 the coupe and roadster models were joined by a 2+2 version of the XK-E, with its wheelbase lengthened by 232 mm and its roof raised by 48 mm. Now a family man with up to two children should not be prevented from buying a Jaguar XK-E, and the narrow, non-folding rear seat bench was made for this purpose in mind, but whoever wanted to transport adults in the back seat had to hope his passengers were not too tall and very limber; but for a short trip, the car was big enough for four.

The XK-E 2+2 was optimistically introduced in New York in April, with the certainty that the greatest interest in this model would once again exist in America. For the first time, it was possible to install a Borg-Warner automatic transmission in the XK-E; since the longer wheelbase provided the room for it, it was limited to the 2+2 model. But this automatic transmission used up so much energy that not much of the sports car's original power remained, especially as the lengthened bodywork had not made it any lighter. With an acceleration of barely nine seconds from zero to 100 kph, the automatic XK-E 2+2 had lost much of its allure, although it was still a fast car. The modified bodywork, longer wheelbase, higher and longer roof, as well as the particularly big windshield and wide doors, did not exactly make the appearance of the XK-E 2+2 any more harmonious. The windows now appeared to be oversize, and the car no longer looked as if it was all one design, but despite all this, it sold rather well, for many customers appreciated the increase in space and comfort.

At the end of 1967 the first XK-E's appeared with minor changes—particularly open headlights—but otherwise they still corresponded to the original type; later they were ranked as "Series One-and-a-half" until, as of October of the following year, all models were sold in fully reworked form as Series Two cars. In them the radiator opening had been enlarged by 68%, two automatically operating ventilators provided for dependable cooling, and for the first time, the car could now be equipped with air conditioning. On account of the new American safety regulations, the bumpers had been extended far around the corners. Bigger brake and back-up lights adorned the rear. Chromed steel wheels were available optionally; the beautiful spoked wheels that were standard equipment had been strengthened, and the center-locking hubcaps had been robbed of their dangerous "nose." On the dashboard, the clock had been removed from the tachometer and was now mounted in the middle, where the light switch had formerly been. Wider switches provided easier operation, and many a corner had lost its sharp angles. It was no longer necessary to press a button to start the car; now there was a modern ignition lock-starter. These were all useful, practical things, but they took away a little of the car's original charm.

The 2+2 had looked somewhat disadvantageous with its oversize, steep windshield, but now the angle had been made sharper, which helped make this model look better. Meeting the American fuel restrictions was a problem that was finally solved by installing two Stromberg CD carburetors, but the performance of these export models sank to about 230 horsepower.

Before Jaguar created a sensation in March of 1971 with the new 12-cylinder Series 3 model, there were still a few more changes made in the interim, such as oleopneumatic shock absorbers to raise the hood, armrests on the doors, and a new ignition system for better cold starting.

At the end of the Fifties, Jaguar had experimented with a twelve-cylinder motor, originally with the intention of building a racing machine for Le Mans. A racing prototype, called the XJ 13 and fitted with a five-liter V-12 motor, had gained the firm some experience, but series production of a V-12 sports car or even a sedan was impossible at that time for reasons of capacity and cost.

The new twelve-cylinder motor making its debut in the Series Three XK-E had a single overhead camshaft on each bank of cylinders and, with 5.3-liter displacement, produced 272 HP at 5850 rpm. The smooth-running motor vibrated very little, was compressedat 9:1, and produced its maximum torque at 400 rpm less than the six-cylinder motor. Many had expected that a new body would be developed for this new motor, but Jaguar limited itself to a few modifications to the still breathlessly beautiful XK-E body.

The big radiator opening of the V-12 had been decorated with a striking chromed grille, and in order to allow mounting wider tires, the new XK-E's now came with clearly widened fenders, which detracted from the appearance of this formerly narrow-looking car. For a short time, not only the V-12 but also a 6-cylinder motor was still available in the Series 3 version, but very few examples of it were built.

The V-12 XK-E was, to be sure, only available as a 2+2 (Fixed Head) or a roadster, the latter sharing the longer wheelbase of the closed version. The two-seat short-chassis coupe was dropped from the production program.

What the last XK-E, with its "face-lift", lost in terms of the formerly treasured primitive quality of the British sports car, it made up for with its fascinating performance. A production Jaguar had never been faster, for with the ability to go from zero to 100 kph in only 6.5 seconds and to 160 kph in 15.5 seconds, The Series 3 XK-E clearly got the better of anything it might meet on the open road. Power steering was now standard, and the Series 3 roadster, thanks to its longer wheelbase, could also be had with automatic transmission.

The prices of these dream cars were still pleasantly modest, and thus more than 7000 of each V-12 type were sold before the 2+2 was dropped in September 1973 and the roadster in February 1975.

The last fifty XK-E roadsters with right-hand drive were—with one exception—painted black and sent, like the majority of their 72,458 predecessors, across the ocean, representing for American collectors and enthusiasts the end of the true Jaguar sports car.

The Era of the XK-E—an often-used designation for the 1961-1975 period—has ended. The first publicly introduced example made its debut at the 1961 Geneva Auto Show. In later chronologies, the production run of this model was listed as "Series 1", and early examples are recognizable at a glance if one looks into the cockpit, where there is plenty of aluminum gleaming on the dashboard. The Series 1 XK-E, with its 3.8 liter dohc motor, remained in production with only slight modifications until October of 1964; most of them were built with left-hand drive as export models.

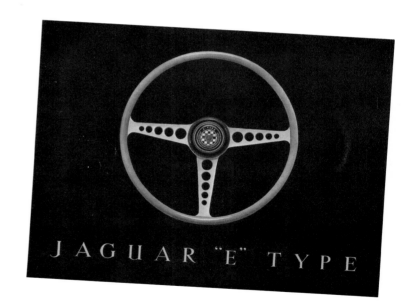

JAGUAR TYP "E" GRAN TURISMO — COUPÉ

Italian-English: The **XK-E** was called a
Gran Turismo in 1961. The illustration
comes from one of the first brochures.

Pages from a German and an American brochure.

JAGUAR TYP "E" GRAN TURISMO—ROADSTER

Abgebildet mit abnehmbarem Fiberglas=Hardtop, welches als Extraaüsrüstung erhältlich ist.

Shown with removable fiberglass hardtop, available as extra
equipment.

NEW 4·2 LITRE 'E' TYPE MODELS

This color page from a catalog
dates from 1964. At right is a
description of the 3.8 liter model.

SPECIFICATIONS

MOTOR. 6 cylinders, 3.8 liter XK motor, Type 'S', with double overhead camshafts, 87 mm bore x 106 mm stroke, displacement 3781 cc. Compression ratio 9:1 (optionally 8:1). Performance (9:1 compression) 268 HP at 5500 rpm. Maximum torque 35.9 mkg at 4000 rpm. Three SU carburetors, Type HD.8, with manual choke. Pressure lubrication by immersed oil pump with mainstream oil filter. Cylinder block of chrome iron alloy with special cylinder liners. Special cylinder head with straight inlets of highly tensile aluminum alloy with hemispherical combustion chambers. Double overhead camshafts, activating large valves at 70-degree angles. Aluminum alloy pistons. Steel connecting rods with big-end bearings of lead-indium alloy. Crankshaft diameter 69.85 mm with counterweights, mounted in 7 large precision bearings of lead-indium alloy. Pressure cooling with thermostatically controlled electrically powered ventilator.

TRANSMISSION. Bevel-geared synchronized 4-speed gearbox with manual shifting and central shift lever. Direct, third and second gears are synchronized. Hydraulic Borg and Beck dry clutch of 25.4 cm diameter. Hardy Spicer driveshaft with hypoid needle bearings. Rear axle with Powr-Lok differential. Rear axle ratio 3.31:1. Optional rear axle ratios: 2.93, 3.7, 3.54. The differential is mounted in the subframe that carries the rear suspension.

FRONT SUSPENSION. Independent front suspension with double transverse links, torsion bars and telescopic shock absorbers. The two lower transverse links are connected by a stabilizer.

REAR SUSPENSION. Independent suspension with a tubular lower transverse link attached movably to the wheel carrier and the subframe next to the differential housing; over it a half-shaft with two cross links. In this way the wheel is held fast in the vertical plane. Longitudinal leading by rubber bushings which attach the subframe to the body, as well as by a longitudinal link between the lower transverse link and an attachment point on the body. Double coil springs with telescopic shock absorbers inside for the center of the suspension. The whole unit including the differential is carried by an easily demountable subframe which is anchored to the body with rubber bushings.

BRAKES. Dunlop special disc brakes with quick-change brake pads on all four wheels. The front-wheel brakes are attached to the wheel hubs, while the rear-wheel brakes are mounted inboard on the half-shafts next to the differential housing. A power brake system is directly linked to the brake pedal. The brake pedal activates two cylinders via an equalizing system, dividing the system into two completely separate brake circuits for the front and rear brakes. The centrally mounted hand brake works on the rear wheels. The brake-fluid warning light on the dashboard is connected to both brake systems.

STEERING. Rack-and-pinion steering. Steering wheel 40.64 mm in diameter, adjustable as to height and distance. From lock to lock 2.75 revolutions. Turning circle 11.27 meters.

WHEELS AND TIRES. Wire-spoke wheels with centrally locking hubcaps and Dunlop RS.5 tires with tubes, size 6.40-15. As optional extra equipment, Dunlop R.5 racing tires, front 6.00-15, rear 6.50-15, are available with suitable special wheels.

FUEL SYSTEM. Lucas electric fuel pump mounted in the fuel tank. Tank capacity 63.6 liters. Fuel filter built into the fuel line in the engine compartment.

ELECTRICAL EQUIPMENT AND INSTRUMENTS. Lucas 12-volt battery, capacity 57 amp/h/10h norm with voltage regulator. Air-cooled generator. Fuse box with 8 clearly marked fuses mounted between the central dashboard panel, which opens for easy access. Side lights. Lucas PL.700 headlights with manual dimmer switch on the dashboard. Separate flasher lever.

Brake taillight, directional light and reflector combined in one housing. Rear license plate light. Directional lights with automatic shutoff and indicator light on the dashboard. Instruments and calibrated operating gauges indirectly lighted via two-stage switch. Reading light. Interior light. Two-tone horn. Three windshield wipers adjustable to two speeds, with automatic switch. Electric windshield washer. Cigarette lighter. Electric starter. Automatic ignition control via vacuum and voltage regulator. Oil-bath coil. Speedometer easy to read, 127 mm diameter with 260 km dial and built-in daily odometer. Electric tachometer, 127 mm diameter, with built-in electric clock. Ammeter. Water temperature gauge. Oil-pressure gauge. Fuel gauge with warning light—all electrically operated. Choke warning light. Combined brake fluid and hand-brake warning light. Cable tube with quickly demountable forward housing section with eight branches, directly linked to the main circuit on the bulkhead.

CHASSIS CONSTRUCTION. Unified all-steel body in monocoque style. The front subframe of square steel tubes carries the weight of the entire powerplant and front suspension as well as the entire front body, which folds forward.

BODY—OPEN TWO-SEATER. Long, streamlined two-door body of low height, with two seats. The folding top of finest mohair has a large rear window mounted on a special frame, making the raising or lowering of the top a simple operation. The folded top is stowed in the interior of the car and covered by a separate removable cover. Removable fiberglass hardtop available as optional extra equipment. The hardtop can be mounted without removing the stowed top. Balanced front hood, opening to the front, guarantees the best access to all mechanical parts. Bowed panoramic windshield and slim side posts offer the best all-around vision. Completely lowering cranked windows. Strong front and rear wraparound bumpers with decorative horns. Two bucket seats, longitudinally adjustable, covered with the finest Vaumol leather and upholstered with thick foam rubber underlays. Three-section dashboard of glare-free matte-finished wood. Plentiful instruments with large tachometer and speedometer in the driver's direct field of vision. The center of the dashboard includes separate oil pressure, water temperature, fuel gauges and ammeter as well as a row of clearly labeled switches to activate the accessory devices. A separate housing under the dashboard is provided for a radio and double loudspeakers (optional extra); there is also a large ashtray mounted in the transmission tunnel. If no radio is mounted, the opening for the controls is covered with a panel. The dashboard on the passenger side includes an uncovered glove compartment as well as a handhold. Three-spoke light metal steering wheel and centrally mounted horn button. Large rear-view mirror with non-glare adjustment. Deep carpets over thick felt underlays. Trunk lid released from inside the car.

HEATER AND DEMISTER. High-performance heater-defroster system with two-stage blower controlled by a switch on the dashboard. Temperature and amount of air onto the windshield and into the interior of the car regulated by a control switch on the dashboard. Direct air ducts to every part of the car.

SPARE WHEEL AND TOOLS. The spare wheel is housed in an easily accessible separate space under the floor of the luggage compartment. The tools including the jack and hubcap hammer are kept in the spare wheel space.

CHANGING TIRES. Centrally located attachment points for the jack on both sides of the car allow simultaneous lifting of two wheels with the help of the special auto jack, which is particularly easy to use.

OVERALL DIMENSIONS. Wheelbase 2438 mm, front and rear track 1270 mm, overall length 4454 mm, overall width 1657 mm, overall height 1222 mm, ground clearance 139 mm, weight (dry) ca. 1123 kg.

JAGUAR TYP "E" GRAN TURISMO—ROAD

It was really a beauty, the Series 1 Roadster. Right: diagrams showing the open and closed car.

A	Radstand	2438	K	Einstieghöhe	406	T	Maximale Kofferraumlänge	1041
B	Überhang, vorne	920	L	Öffnungsweise der Türe	822	U	Windschutzscheibenbreite	1270
C	Überhang, hinten	1095	M	Sitzhöhe	203	V	Windschutzscheibenhöhe	457
D	Gesamtlänge	4454	N	Sitztiefe	508	W	Spurweite, vorne	1270
E	Gesamtbreite	1657	O	Sitzbreite	457	X	Spurweite, hinten	1270
F	Gesamthöhe	1222	P	Innenbreite in Schulterhöhe	1244	Y	Kopfraum	889
G	Bodenabstand	139	Q	Abstand Lenkrad – Sitzlehne	432	Z	Bodenabstand, vordere Stoßstange	425
H	Freiwinkel, vorne	21	R	Abstand Pedale – Sitzpolster	457	AA	Bodenabstand, hintere Stoßstange	546
J	Freiwinkel, hinten	21	S	Maximale Kofferraumbreite	990	BB	Türöffnungswinkel	65
						CC	Abstand Boden – obere Türkante	1137

Alle Abmessungen sind in Millimetern angegeben und beziehen sich auf ein belastetes Fahrzeug.

A	Radstand	2438	K	Einstieghöhe	406	T	Maximale Kofferraumlänge	1041
B	Überhang, vorne	920	L	Öffnungsweise der Türe	822	U	Windschutzscheibenbreite	1270
C	Überhang, hinten	1095	M	Sitzhöhe	203	V	Windschutzscheibenhöhe	457
D	Gesamtlänge	4454	N	Sitztiefe	508	W	Spurweite, vorne	1270
E	Gesamtbreite	1657	O	Sitzbreite	457	X	Spurweite, hinten	1270
F	Gesamthöhe	1222	P	Innenbreite in Schulterhöhe	1244	Y	Kopfraum	889
G	Bodenabstand	139	Q	Abstand Lenkrad – Sitzlehne	432	Z	Bodenabstand, vordere Stoßstange	425
H	Freiwinkel, vorne	21	R	Abstand Pedale – Sitzpolster	457	AA	Bodenabstand, hintere Stoßstange	546
J	Freiwinkel, hinten	21	S	Maximale Kofferraumbreite	990	BB	Türöffnungswinkel	65
						CC	Abstand Boden – obere Türkante	1137

Alle Abmessungen sind in Millimetern angegeben und beziehen sich auf ein belastetes Fahrzeug.

Bezeichnet abnehmbares Hard Top.

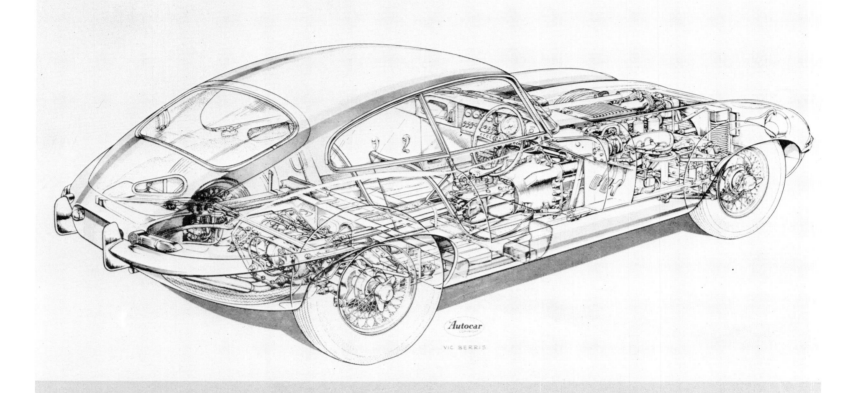

JAGUAR TYP "E" GRAN TURISMO — COUPÉ

*Diese Phantomzeichnung des Coupé Modelles ist mit Genehmigung von
'The Autocar' widergegeben und vermittelt einen Überblick über
die Konstruktionsmerkmale und allgemeinen technischen Einzelheiten.*

This cutaway drawing of the Coupe is reproduced with the permission of
'The Autocar' and affords an overview of the construction features and
general technical details.

These drawings also came from a 1961 catalog. Reference is made to publication in the auto magazine THE AUTOCAR and even includes a complete test page, which was published on March 24, 1961—just a few days before the introduction of the XK-E.

JAGUAR E-TYPE GRAND TOURING COUPE

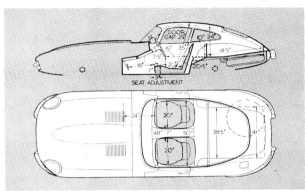

Scale ⅛in. to 1ft. Driving seat in central position. Cushions uncompressed.

DATA

PRICE (basic), with fixed head coupé body, £1,550.
British purchase tax, £646 19s 2d.
Total (in Great Britain), £2,196 19s 2d.
Extras: Chromium plated wire wheels, £60 4s 2d inc. P.T. Dunlop R.5 racing tyres: price to be announced later.

ENGINE: Capacity, 3,781 c.c. (230·6 cu. in.).
Number of cylinders, 6.
Bore and stroke, 87 × 106 mm (3·42 × 4·17in.).
Valve gear, twin overhead camshafts.
Compression ratio, 9 to 1.
B.h.p., 265 (gross) at 5,500 r.p.m. (b.h.p. per ton laden 195·4).
Torque, 260 lb. ft. at 4,000 r.p.m.
M.p.h. per 1,000 r.p.m. in top gear, 23·0 R.S.5; 24·6 R.5.

WEIGHT (with 5 gal fuel): 24·1 cwt (2,702lb).
Weight distribution (per cent): F, 49·6; R, 50·4.
Laden as tested, 27·1 cwt (3,038 lb).
Lb per c.c. (laden), 0·80.

BRAKES: Dunlop discs, inboard at rear. Hydraulic with vacuum servo, separate systems front and rear.
Disc diameter: F, 11in.; R, 10in.
Swept area: F, 242 sq. in.; R, 219 sq. in. (340 sq. in. per ton laden).

TYRES: 6·40 × 15in. Dunlop R.S.5.
Pressures (p.s.i.): F, 23; R, 25 (normal). F, 30; R, 35 (fast driving).
(Optional) Dunlop R.5: F (6·00 × 15in.), 35; R (6·00 × 15in.), 40 (maximum speeds).

TANK CAPACITY: 14 Imperial gallons (63·6 litres).
Oil sump, 11 pints (6·2 litres).
Cooling system, 22 pints (12·5 litres).

DIMENSIONS: Wheelbase, 8ft 0in. (243·8 cm).
Track: 4ft 2in. (127 cm).
Length (overall): 14ft 7·3in. (445·8 cm).
Width: 5ft 5·2in. (165·6cm).
Height: 4ft 0in. (122cm).
Ground clearance, 5·0in. (12·7cm).
Frontal area, 15 sq. ft. (approximately).

ELECTRICAL SYSTEM: 12-volt; 57 ampère-hour battery.
Headlamps, 60-60 watt bulbs.

SUSPENSION: Front, wishbones, torsion bars, telescopic dampers.
Rear, independent, transverse tubular and trailing links, twin coil springs and telescopic dampers each side, anti-roll bar.

PERFORMANCE

ACCELERATION TIMES (mean):
Speed range, Gear Ratios, and Time in Sec.

m.p.h.	3·31 to 1	4·25 to 1	6·16 to 1	11·18 to 1
10—30	—	—	3·2	1·9
20—40	5·5	4·3	2·8	1·9
30—50	5·4	4·3	2·8	—
40—60	5·5	4·3	3·0	—
50—70	5·4	4·1	3·1	—
60—80	5·6	4·1	—	—
70—90	5·8	4·5	—	—
80—100	6·1	4·9	—	—
90—110	6·3	6·0	—	—
100—120	7·2	—	—	—
110—130	8·5	—	—	—

From rest through gears to:

30 m.p.h.	..	2·8 sec
40 ,,	..	4·4 ,,
50 ,,	..	5·6 ,,
60 ,,	..	6·9 ,,
70 ,,	..	8·5 ,,
80 ,,	..	11·1 ,,
90 ,,	..	13·2 ,,
100 ,,	..	16·2 ,,
110 ,,	..	19·2 ,,
120 ,,	..	25·9 ,,
130 ,,	..	33·1 ,,

Standing quarter mile 14·7 sec.

MAXIMUM SPEEDS ON GEARS (R.5 tyres):

Gear		m.p.h.	k.p.h.
Top	(mean)	150·4	242·1
	(best)	151·7	244·2
3rd	.. ..	116	187
2nd	.. ..	78	125
1st	.. ..	42	68

TRACTIVE EFFORT (by Tapley meter):

		Pull (lb per ton)	Equivalent gradient
Top ..	..	360	1 in 6·1
Third	..	520	1 in 4·2
Second	..	755	1 in 2·8

BRAKES (at 30 m.p.h. in neutral)

Pedal load in lb	Retardation	Equiv. stopping distance in ft
25	0·20g	151
50	0·43g	70
75	0·64g	47
100	0·84g	36
115	0·87g	34·7

FUEL CONSUMPTION: (at steady speeds)

		Top Gear
30 m.p.h.		32·0 m.p.g.
40	,,	32·5 ,,
50	,,	30·5 ,,
60	,,	28·2 ,,
70	,,	26·5 ,,
80	,,	24·5 ,,
90	,,	22·5 ,,
100	,,	19·0 ,,
110	,,	16·5 ,,

Overall fuel consumption for 1,891 miles, 17·9 m.p.g. (15·8 litres per 100 km).
Approximate normal range 16-21 m.p.g. (17·6-13·5 litres per 100 km).
Fuel: Super Premium.

TEST CONDITIONS: Weather: Dry, sunny, still air for maximum speed runs.
Air temperature, 41·7 deg. F.
Model described 17 March 1961.

STEERING: Turning circle:
Between kerbs: R, 40ft 5in.; L, 38ft 5in.
Between walls: R, 42ft 0in.; L, 40ft 0in.
Turns of steering wheel lock to lock, 2·75.

SPEEDOMETER: m.p.h.

		10	20	30	40	50	60	70	80	90	100	110	120	130	136
Car speedometer	..	10	20	30	40	50	60	70	80	90	100	110	120	130	136
True Speed. R. 5s	..	11	22	32	42	52	62	72	83	93	104	115	126	—	—
True Speed. R.S. 5s	..	10	20	30	44	51	61	72	82	92	102	113	124	135	140

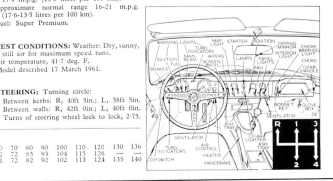

XK-E ROADSTER

Twin bucket seats, adjustable for reach, upholstered in finest leather over foam rubber; adjustable three-spoke steering wheel of polished lightweight alloy, with wood rim; wind-up windows; console for radio and twin speakers.

Interchangeable hard or soft convertible top. Three section instrument panel, with r.p.m. counter, 160 m.p.h. speedometer; oil pressure, water temperature and fuel gauges; fuel and brake fluid warning lights.

This small, barely postcard-size brochure for the American market appeared in 1964. Here the car was called the XK-E. Along with the 3.8 liter XK-E, the 3.8 liter Mark II and luxury Mark X sedan were also in production.

PARTS FOR YOUR JAGUAR

Jaguar Cars Inc., U. S. subsidiary of Jaguar Cars Ltd., of Coventry, England, wishes to call attention to the fact that Jaguar was one of the first imported motor cars to be sold in the United States in significant numbers.

In the early 1950's, therefore, Jaguar began an intensive study of ways and means of ensuring an adequate supply of parts to its Distributors and Dealers and, finally, to Jaguar owners in North America.

Jaguar Cars Inc. is proud to say that its prolonged efforts to improve the direct flow of parts from factory to point-of-service have achieved gratifying results.

Today, Jaguar Distributors and Dealers carry parts stocks ample to furnish service to the Jaguar cars registered in their territories. A factory Parts Depot is located in Long Island City, only minutes away from the major airline terminals of New York. A similar Parts Depot is maintained in Canada by Jaguar Cars (Canada) Ltd.

Time, energies and expense have not been spared by Jaguar in trying to provide Jaguar owners with the highest standard of service available to an imported car driver in the continent of North America.

That interested the Americans very much—the question of whether enough spare parts were in stock in the USA. It was said that everything was available from Jaguar Cars Inc. in Long Island City, New York.

JAGUAR XK-E ROADSTER

By victory after victory on the racetracks of the world, Jaguar has earned for itself a position in the very front rank of modern sports cars.

Five times winners at Le Mans, three times victors at Rheims, several times winners of the R. A. C. Tourist Trophy and victorious in innumerable other International and National events, the racetrack breeding of Jaguar is evident from the moment the wheel is handled.

All the accumulated wealth of knowledge and experience gained in the hard school of motor racing have been built into the new XK-E Jaguar models, one of the fastest production sports cars ever offered for public sale.

XK-E models are equipped with 3.8 litre twin overhead camshaft XK engines, with three carburetors, developing 265 b. h. p. at 5,500 r. p. m.'s, with straight port cylinder heads of high tensile aluminum alloy and with hemispherical combustion chambers.

These engines provide a new high level of performance, yet, notwithstanding the high speed potential of the XK-E, the Jaguar characteristics of smoothness, silence, tractability and road adhesion are such that complete and effortless mastery is in the hands of the driver at all times and at all speeds.

The construction of the XK-E is unique, since it comprises a stressed shell, all-steel body of patented monocoque construction, which was developed and proven in the famous "D" Type Jaguar competition car in many of the world's most grueling races.

This form of construction has made it possible to reduce weight drastically, without compromising strength or rigidity. The XK-E is, therefore, approximately 600 pounds lighter than its predecessor, which makes this car capable of truly outstanding performance.

The two-door, two-seater bodies possess extremely low drag

Twin bucket seats, adjustable for reach, upholstered in finest leather over foam rubber; adjustable three-spoke steering wheel of polished lightweight alloy, with wood rim; wind-up windows; console for radio and twin speakers.

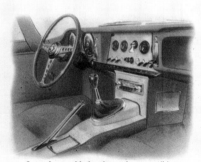

Interchangeable hard or soft convertible top. Three section instrument panel, with R.P.M. Counter, 160 m.p.h. speedometer; oil pressure, water temperature and fuel gauges; fuel and brake fluid warning lights.

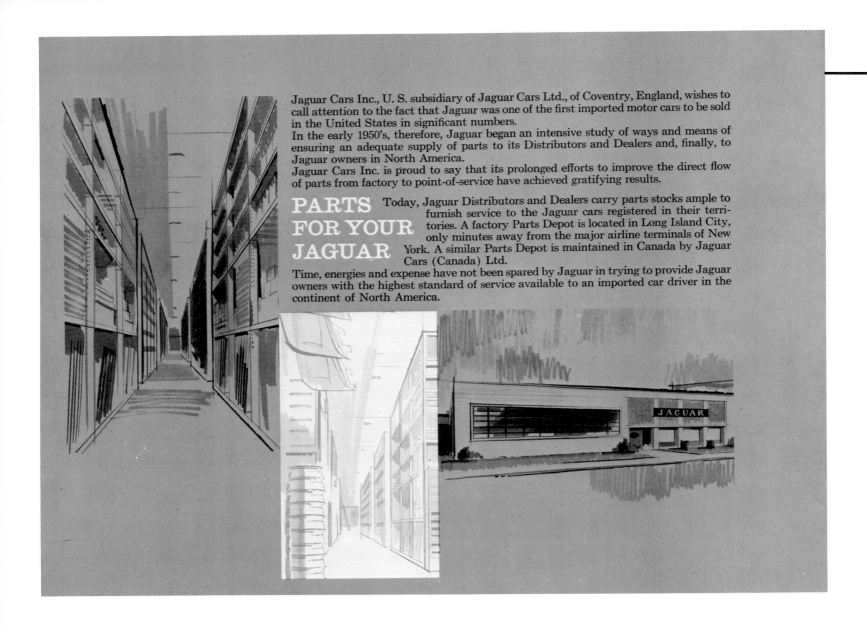

Jaguar Cars Inc., U. S. subsidiary of Jaguar Cars Ltd., of Coventry, England, wishes to call attention to the fact that Jaguar was one of the first imported motor cars to be sold in the United States in significant numbers.

In the early 1950's, therefore, Jaguar began an intensive study of ways and means of ensuring an adequate supply of parts to its Distributors and Dealers and, finally, to Jaguar owners in North America.

Jaguar Cars Inc. is proud to say that its prolonged efforts to improve the direct flow of parts from factory to point-of-service have achieved gratifying results.

PARTS FOR YOUR JAGUAR

Today, Jaguar Distributors and Dealers carry parts stocks ample to furnish service to the Jaguar cars registered in their territories. A factory Parts Depot is located in Long Island City, only minutes away from the major airline terminals of New York. A similar Parts Depot is maintained in Canada by Jaguar Cars (Canada) Ltd.

Time, energies and expense have not been spared by Jaguar in trying to provide Jaguar owners with the highest standard of service available to an imported car driver in the continent of North America.

Grace, Space, Pace

The slogan expressing the car's sleek good looks, roominess and progress was certainly appropriate for the XK-E. The car was given a 4.2 liter motor in 1964, offering the same power but superb torque. The car made many friends right away.

NEW ADVANCED XK ENGINE
4.2 litre, 6 cylinder, twin overhead camshaft advanced design of race-proved 3 carburetter Jaguar XK engine, five times winner of Le Mans, gives higher torque for increased acceleration and flexibility.

NEW ALL SYNCHROMESH GEARBOX
Four-speed all synchro crash-proof transmission gives smooth, rapid changes. New diaphragm spring clutch gives lighter pedal pressure and long life.

NEW EFFORTLESS BRAKING
New brake servo gives lower effort and greater power for the disc brakes on all four wheels. Separate fluid systems for front and rear give added safety.

The first catalog for the new XK-E with 4.2 liter motor, published in October of 1964.

JAGUAR

BY APPOINTMENT
TO H.M. QUEEN ELIZABETH
THE QUEEN MOTHER
MOTOR CAR MANUFACTURERS
JAGUAR CARS LTD

Grace...Space...Pace

The
4·2 LITRE 'E' TYPE JAGUAR

In response to a world wide demand, Jaguar proudly introduce into the present range a more powerful model which, whilst retaining the characteristics—aerodynamic body, disc brakes and independent suspension on all four wheels, which have made the 'E' type world famous, embodies many new technical advancements combining to give maximum performance with saloon car comfort.

A new 4.2 litre XK engine of advanced design steps up performance to an entirely new level and, together with the new all synchromesh gearbox, New effortless braking, New alternator, Pre-engaged starter, New "shaped" seating, still further improves that " special kind of motoring which no other car in the world can offer."

NEW ALTERNATOR gives greatly increased current supply over wide range of engine speeds, ensuring adequate current supply—even with city driving—for the extensive electrical service embodied.

PRE-ENGAGED STARTER facilitates starting under conditions of extreme cold.

SHAPED SEATING designed for maximum comfort, and upholstered in finest quality Vaumol leather over Dunlopillo foam rubber cushions.

SPECIFICATIONS

ENGINE. 6 cylinder, twin overhead camshaft, 4.2 litre XK Jaguar engine. 92.07 mm. bore, 106 mm. stroke (3.625" by 4.1732"), cubic capacity 4235 c.c. (258.43 cu. in.). Compression ratio 9 : 1 (8 : 1 optional). Power output (9 : 1) 265 b.h.p. at 5400 r.p.m., torque 283 ft./lb. at 4,000 r.p.m. Three S.U. carburetters, Type HD.8 with manual choke control. Forced lubrication by submerged pump system incorporating a full flow filter. Chrome iron cylinder block fitted with dry type cylinder liners. Special 'straight port' cylinder head of high tensile aluminium alloy featuring hemispherical combustion chambers and twin overhead camshafts operating large valves of 70° included angle. Aluminium alloy pistons. Steel connecting rods fitted with lead indium big end bearings. 2¾ ins. diameter counterweighted crankshaft carried on seven large lead indium bearings. Pressurised cooling system with thermostatically controlled, electrically driven fan.

TRANSMISSION. Manually operated four speed, single helical all synchromesh gearbox. Ratios: Top 3.07, 3rd. 3.90, 2nd. 5.34, 1st. 8.23, Reverse 9.45. Centrally positioned change speed lever. Baulk ring synchromesh on all four forward ratios. Laycock Hausserman 10" diaphragm clutch. Hardy Spicer needle bearing propeller shaft. Hypoid rear axle fitted with limited slip differential. Ratio 3.07 : 1. Optional ratios 3.31, 3.54. Differential unit mounted in sub-frame carrying the rear suspension.

SUSPENSION—FRONT. Independent front suspension incorporating transverse wishbones and torsion bars controlled by telescopic hydraulic dampers. Anti-roll bar fitted to lower wishbones.

SUSPENSION—REAR. Fully independent rear suspension incorporating, on each side, a lower transverse tubular link pivotted at the wheel carrier and subframe adjacent to the differential case and above this, a halfshaft universally jointed at each end. These serve to locate the wheel in a transverse plane. Longitudinal location is provided by the rubber mountings locating the sub-assembly in the body structure and by a radius arm between the lower link and a mounting point on the body structure. Twin coil springs, each enclosing a telescopic damper, provide the suspension medium. The whole assembly together with the differential unit is carried in an easily detachable sub-frame which is located in the body structure by rubber mountings

BRAKES. Dunlop bridge-type disc brakes featuring quick-change pads, are fitted to all four wheels. Front brakes fitted on wheel hubs, rear brakes fitted inboard on half shafts adjacent to differential unit. Suspended-vacuum type servo operated by tandem master cylinder system divided into two entirely independent hydraulic systems to front and rear brakes. Centrally positioned handbrake operates on rear wheels only. Brake fluid level warning light operates on both systems.

STEERING. Rack and pinion. 16 ins. steering wheel with separate adjustments for height and reach. Number of turns lock to lock 2¾. Turning circle 37 ft. diameter.

WHEELS AND TYRES. Wire spoke wheels with centre lock hubs fitted with Dunlop 6.40 × 15 type RS.5 tyres and tubes. Dunlop R.5 racing tyres available as optional equipment. 6.00 × 15 front. 6.50 × 15 rear on special wheels.

FUEL SUPPLY. By S.U. electric pump. Tank of 14 Imperial gallon capacity. Petrol filter incorporated into fuel line and located in engine compartment.

ELECTRICAL EQUIPMENT, INSTRUMENTS AND FITTINGS. Lucas alternator generator. 12 volt negative earth system. Large capacity battery giving 57 amp-hours at 10 hour rate with current voltage control. Eight fuse control box, fully labelled, located behind hinged central facia panel for ease of access. Side lamps. Lucas sealed beam, asymmetric dip, headlamps with hand-operated dipping control on facia. Separate lever actuating headlamp flashing. Separate stop-tail direction and reflector units mounted in a single assembly. Rear number plate lamps. Flashing direction indicators with self-cancellation and warning light on facia. Instruments and labelled switches illuminated by internal floodlighting controlled by a two-position dimmer switch. Map reading light. Interior light. Twin-blended note horns. Triple blade two-speed self-parking windscreen wiper unit. Electrically operated windscreen washers. Cigar lighter with luminous socket. Starter motor. Vacuum and centrifugal automatic ignition control. Oil coil ignition. 5 ins. diameter 160 m.p.h. speedometer incorporating total and trip distance recorders. 5 ins. diameter electrically operated revolution counter incorporating an electric clock. Ammeter . Electrically operated water temperature gauge, oil pressure gauge, fuel gauge with low level warning light. Choke warning light. Combined handbrake and brake fluid low level warning light. Wiring harness in quickly detachable front body section connected to main circuits through an eight-pin connector mounted on engine compartment bulkhead.

BODY CONSTRUCTION. Stressed shell steel body of unique patented, monocoque construction. Front sub-frame of square section steel tubing carries engine unit, suspension and forward hinged front section.

BODY—OPEN TWO SEATER. Two door two seater body of extremely low drag characteristics resulting from intensive wind tunnel testing. The folding hood incorporating a large rear window is of finest quality mohair, mounted on a special frame to permit single handed erection or stowing. When stowed the hood assembly is completely concealed by a separate detachable cover. Fibreglass detachable hardtop available as an optional extra.

OPEN AND FIXED HEAD COUPE. Counterbalanced, forward opening front section provides excellent accessibility to all mechanical components. Wrapround windscreen and thin pillars provide superb forward visibility. Door lights completely concealed within doors when fully lowered. Wrapround bumpers with overriders at front and rear. Twin bucket seats, adjustable for reach and rake, upholstered in finest quality Vaumol leather over Dunlopillo foam rubber cushions. Three panel facia. Facia and screen rail in matt grained finish to eliminate reflection. Comprehensive instrumentation with revolution counter and speedometer positioned in front of driver. Central panel contains separate fuel gauge and ammeter, together with a row of labelled tumbler switches controlling ancillary equipment. Separate housing beneath panel contains a radio and twin speakers (optional extra) together with an ashtray. When no radio is fitted, the speaker grilles are retained and the radio control panel aperture is blanked off with an escutcheon. Panel in front of passenger contains an open-fronted glove compartment and grab handle. Three-spoke, polished alloy, lightweight steering wheel with wood rim and central horn push. Wide angle vertically adjustable rear view mirror incorporating anti-dazzle secondary mirror position. Deep pile carpets over thick felt underlay. Luggage accommodation provided in tail of car. Luggage boot lid controlled from inside the car.

HEATING AND DEMISTING. High output fresh air heating and multi-point windscreen demisting system incorporating a two-speed fan controlled by switch on facia. Temperature and volume of air to windscreen and car interior regulated by controls mounted on facia panel. Ducts direct air to each side of compartment.

SPARE WHEEL AND TOOLS. The spare wheel is carried beneath the boot floor in a separate compartment and is readily accessible. The tools, in a special fitted and lined container, are housed in the spare wheel compartment.

JACKING. Centrally located jacking sockets enable the front and rear wheels on either side of the car to be raised simultaneously by means of the manually-operated screw type easy lift jack.

PRINCIPAL DIMENSIONS. Wheelbase, 8 ft. 0 ins. Track, front and rear, 4 ft. 2 ins. Overall length, 14 ft. 7 5/16 ins. Overall width, 5 ft. 5¼ ins. Overall height, 4 ft. 0 ins. Ground clearance (laden) 5½ ins. Dry weight (approx.) 22½ cwts.

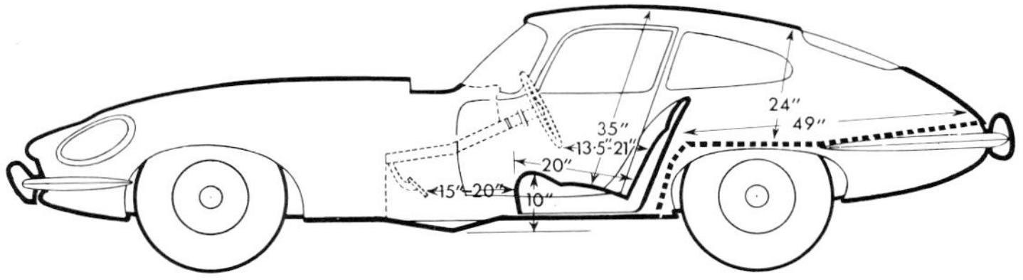

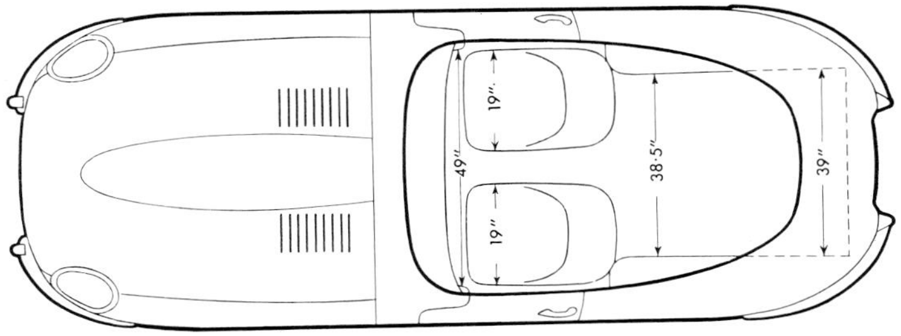

J A G U A R   C A R S   L T D · C O V E N T R Y · E N G L A N D

The issue of this catalogue does not constitute an offer. Jaguar Cars Ltd., reserve the right to amend specifications without notice.

Printed in England by W. W. Curtis Ltd. Coventry

It looks roomier than it really is. And if one filled the luggage space of the coupe, the view to the rear was blocked.

The Series 2 XK-E offered a number of modifications but had the same 4.2 liter motor as its predecessor. In the USA the car was still called the XK-E.

A folded brochure to introduce the Series 2 XK-E, here again for customers in the USA. Four out of five cars of this type too were exported, generally to America.

JAGUAR XK-E 1968

1968 is anniversary year for Jaguar cars. For twenty years now Jaguars have been sold in America in quantity. A few were indeed imported each year before that, even in the Thirties. But it was in 1948 that the famous XK120 Jaguar was first unveiled at the London motor show and soon Americans were buying them in thousands. American sportsmen became great enthusiasts for the Jaguar and many of them still treasure vintage examples of the succeeding types—XK120M, XK140, XK150, XK150S.

By that time—ten years ago—Jaguar had also built the famous C- and D-type sports racing cars, five times winners at Le Mans. From these came the formidable XK-SS and finally in 1961 the first of the E-type series.

All these great cars—both those sold to the public and the racing cars—had similar engines, that is with six-cylinders in line and twin overhead camshafts, but of widely varied size. The first E-types had 3.8 litre engines but the latest versions all have Jaguar's largest 4.2 litre and many other advanced design features listed overleaf.

So this is anniversary year for Jaguar, anniversary of the introduction of some of the world's great cars, culminating in the superb, exciting 1968 XK-E models. (Prices from $5,372 POE)

Twenty years of marketing by Jaguar in America also brings to customers an established, experienced distributor/dealer sales and service organization throughout the U.S.A.

Jaguar Cars Inc., 32 East 57th Street, New York, N.Y. 10022

ROADSTER

COUPE

JAGUAR

2+2

Excerpts from a 1968 brochure. The seating arrangements in the Two Plus Two appear quite spacious here . . .

EFFORTLESS GEAR SELECTION. Automatic models have central, floor mounted gear selector with simple fore and aft movement giving instant and effortless control over the operation of the gearbox and manual override if required.

BRAKING. Disc brakes on all four wheels. Vacuum servo ensures smooth, effortless braking with a light, progressive pedal. Independent hydraulic systems for front and rear brakes provide maximum safety.

ALTERNATOR. Alternator gives high current supply over wide range of engine speeds thus ensuring adequate current supply, even when driving in city traffic.

Above: Technical features of the Series 2 XK-E: Automatic transmission (optional), front and rear disc brakes, AC generator.

JAGUAR IN ACTION

A small-format but inclusive two-color brochure. On the last two interior pages, the addresses of 81 Jaguar service representatives in West Germany are listed.

JAGUAR

„E" 2+2

COUPE

Sehr schnelles, geräumiges
GT-Fahrzeug

MOTOR: Sechszylinder „XK"-Motor mit zwei obenliegenden Nockenwellen und drei Vergasern. Verdichtung 9 : 1, Bohrung 92,07 mm × Hub 106 mm. Zylinderinhalt 4235 ccm; 265 PS bei 5500 U/min; 39 mkg bei 4000 U/min. Thermostatisch gesteuerter, elektrisch betriebener Ventilator.

GETRIEBE: Vollsynchronisiertes Vierganggetriebe. Knüppelschaltung. Gegen Aufpreis vollautomatisches Getriebe (Hydr. Drehmomentwandler und 3-Gang-Planetengetriebe) mit zwei Fahrbereichen (D 1 / D 2), von denen einer wahlweise auch geschaltet werden kann.

RADAUFHÄNGUNG: Vorn Dreieckquerlenker und Längstorsionsstabfedern. Kurvenstabilisator vorn und hinten. Hinten Einzelradaufhängung mit gegabelten Führungsarmen, Halbachsen mit je 2 Universalgelenken und Längslenkern sowie je 2 Schraubenfedern mit innenliegenden Teleskopstoßdämpfern. Dies ist in einem leicht demontierbaren Hilfsrahmen zusammengefaßt, der durch Gummiaufhängungen mit der Karosserie verbunden ist.

BREMSEN: Zweikreis-Vierradscheibenbremsen mit Bremshilfe, selbstnachstellend.
Handbremse, selbstnachstellend, wirkt mechanisch auf die Hinterräder.

LENKUNG: Zahnstangenlenkung. 2,85 Umdrehungen von Anschlag zu Anschlag. Verstellbare Lenkradsäule.

RÄDER UND BEREIFUNG: Speichenräder mit Zentralverschluß 185×15 mit Schlauch.

KRAFTSTOFFVERSORGUNG: Elektrische Benzinpumpe. Tankinhalt 65 Liter.

ELEKTR. AUSRÜSTUNG UND INSTRUMENTE: Wechselstromlichtmaschine, 12-Volt-Anlage, Rückfahrscheinwerfer, Scheibenwischer mit zwei Stufen, Scheibenwaschanlage, Lichthupe, Tourenzähler, Amperemeter, Uhr, Zigarrenanzünder etc.

KAROSSERIE: Selbsttragend, der vordere Teil ist ein leicht demontierbarer Vierkantstahlrohrrahmen, 2-türig, 2 Sitze sowie 2 Notsitze; der Kofferraum kann durch eine dritte Tür be- und entladen werden. Lederpolsterung. Veloursteppiche. Reserverad und Werkzeug befinden sich unter dem Kofferraumboden.

HEIZUNG UND BELÜFTUNG: Frischluft-Heizungssystem mit fünf Defrosterdüsen und zweistufigem Gebläse. Für die Vordersitze ist diese Anlage getrennt regulierbar.

HAUPTABMESSUNGEN: Radstand 267 cm, Spur vorn 127 cm, Spur hinten 127 cm, Länge 478 cm, Breite 166 cm, Höhe 127 cm, Wendekreis 12,3 m.

JAGUAR "E" 2+2 COUPE
Very fast, roomy GT vehicle

MOTOR: Six-cylinder "XK" motor with dual overhead camshafts and three carburetors. Compression 9:1. Bore 92.07 mm x stroke 106 mm. Displacement 4235 cc. 265 HP at 5500 rpm, 39 mkg torque at 4000 rpm. Thermostatically controlled electric cooling.

TRANSMISSION: Fully synchronized four-speed gearbox, stick shift. Fully automatic transmission at extra charge (hydraulic torque converter and 3-speed planetary drive) with two drive speeds (D1·D2), either one of which may be chosen.

SUSPENSION: Front transverse wishbone links and longitudinal torsion bars. Front and rear antiroll bars. Independent rear suspension with forked leading arms, half-axles, each with two universal joints and longitudinal links plus two coil springs each with telescopic shock absorbers inside. This is mounted in an easily demountable subframe which is attached to the body by rubber bushings.

BRAKES: Two-circuit four-wheel disc brakes, self-adjusting. Hand brake, self-adjusting, operating mechanically on the rear wheels.

STEERING: Rack-and-pinion steering, 2.85 turns from lock to lock. Adjustable steering column.

WHEELS AND TIRES: Spoked wheels with central hubcaps, 185x15 tires with tubes.

FUEL SUPPLY: Electric fuel pump. Tank capacity 65 liters.

ELECTRICAL EQUIPMENT AND INSTRUMENTS: AC generator, 12-volt system, back-up lights, two-speed windshield wiper, windshield washer system, flashers, odometer, ammeter, clock, lighter etc.

BODY: Self-bearing, the front is an easily demountable steel tube frame, two doors, two seats plus two occasional seats, the luggage compartment can be loaded and unloaded through a third door. Leather upholstery, velour carpets, spare wheel and tools are under the luggage compartment floor.

HEATING AND COOLING: Fresh-air heating system with five defroster ducts and two-stage blower. This system is separately controllable for the two front seats.

PRINCIPAL DIMENSIONS: Wheelbase 267 cm, front track 127 cm, rear track 127 cm, length 478 cm, width 166 cm, height 127 cm, turning circle 12.3 meters.

MOTOR: Sechszylinder „XK"-Motor mit zwei obenliegenden Nockenwellen und drei Vergasern. Verdichtung 9 : 1, Bohrung 92,07 mm × Hub 106 mm. Zylinderinhalt 4235 ccm; 265 PS bei 5500 U/min; 39 mkg bei 4000 U/min. Thermostatisch gesteuerter, elektrisch betriebener Ventilator.

GETRIEBE: Vollsynchronisiertes Vierganggetriebe.' Knüppelschaltung.

RADAUFHÄNGUNG: Vorn Dreieckquerlenker und Längstorsionsstabfedern. Kurvenstabilisator vorn und hinten. Hinten Einzelradaufhängung mit gegabelten Führungsarmen, Halbachsen mit je 2 Universalgelenken und Längslenkern sowie je 2 Schraubenfedern mit innenliegenden Teleskopstoßdämpfern. Dies ist in einem leicht demontierbaren Hilfsrahmen zusammengefaßt, der durch Gummiaufhängungen mit der Karosserie verbunden ist.

BREMSEN: Zweikreis-Vierradscheibenbremsen mit Bremshilfe, selbstnachstellend.
Handbremse, selbstnachstellend, wirkt mechanisch auf die Hinterräder.

LENKUNG: Zahnstangenlenkung. 2,5 Umdrehungen von Anschlag zu Anschlag. Verstellbare Lenkradsäule.

RÄDER UND BEREIFUNG: Speichenräder mit Zentralverschluß 185×15 mit Schlauch.

KRAFTSTOFFVERSORGUNG: Elektrische Benzinpumpe. Tankinhalt 65 Liter.

ELEKTR. AUSRÜSTUNG UND INSTRUMENTE: Wechselstromlichtmaschine, 12-Volt-Anlage, Rückfahrscheinwerfer, Scheibenwischer mit zwei Stufen, Scheibenwaschanlage, Lichthupe, Tourenzähler, Amperemeter, Uhr, Zigarrenanzünder etc.

KAROSSERIE: Selbsttragend, der vordere Teil ist ein leicht demontierbarer Vierkantstahlrohrrahmen, 2-türig, 2 Plätze, versenkbares Roadsterverdeck mit großem Rückfenster. Lederpolsterung, Veloursteppiche. Gegen Aufpreis auswechselbares Hard-Top. Reserverad und Werkzeug befinden sich unter dem Kofferraumboden.

HEIZUNG UND BELÜFTUNG: Frischluft-Heizungssystem mit fünf Defrosterdüsen und zweistufigem Gebläse.

HAUPTABMESSUNGEN: Radstand 244 cm, Spur vorn 127 cm, Spur hinten 127 cm, Länge 445 cm, Breite 166 cm, Höhe 122 cm, Wendekreis 11,3 m.

JAGUAR

„E"

ROADSTER

Sehr schnelles GT-Fahrzeug

Data similar to page 36.

"Very fast GT vehicle"— simple, placed in space, formulated in dry English style. This idyll at a mountain lake seems more contemplative than dynamic.

Jaguar 'E' Type range Series 2

OPEN 2-SEATER (AND OPTIONAL HARD TOP)

PRINCIPAL DIMENSIONS: Wheelbase, 8 ft. 0 ins.; Track, front and rear, 4 ft. 2 ins.; Overall length, 14 ft. $7\frac{5}{16}$ ins.; Overall width, 5 ft. $5\frac{1}{4}$ ins.; Overall height, 4 ft. 0 ins.; Ground clearance (laden), $5\frac{1}{2}$ ins.; Turning circle 37 ft.; Fuel tank capacity 14 imp. gallons.

Series 2 Features

ENGINEERING:

● 4.2 litre, 6 cylinder, twin overhead camshaft three carburetter 265 b.h.p. 'XK' engine giving high power and torque output for maximum acceleration and flexibility of top gear performance, and providing low fuel consumption.

● Four speed all synchromesh gearbox with improvements for smoother, quieter running.

● Diaphragm-spring clutch requiring only light pedal pressure.

● Optional automatic transmission (2 2 model only).

● Fully independent suspension of all four wheels.

● Servo-assisted disc brakes on all four wheels, with quick-change pads.

● Independent hydraulic circuits to front and rear brakes.

● Wide section tyres for maximum adhesion.

● Collapsible steering column, fitted with energy-absorbing sleeve.

● Rack and pinion, power assisted steering (optional extra).

In 1968, of course, Jaguar belonged to the Leyland firm, as the emblem at the upper right indicates, and just as clearly it was indicated that they were suppliers to the English court.

Jaguar 'E' Type range Series 2

SERIES 2 'E' TYPE OPEN 2-SEATER (and optional Hard Top Model)

ENGINE. 6 cylinder, twin overhead camshaft, 4.2 litre XK Jaguar engine. 92.07 mm. bore, 106 mm. stroke (3.625" by 4.1732"), cubic capacity 4235 c.c. (258.43 cu. in.). Compression ratio 9 : 1 (8 : 1 optional) Power output (9 : 1) 265 b.h.p. at 5400 r.p.m., torque 283 ft./lb. at 4,000 r.p.m. Three S.U. carburetters, Type HD.8 with manual choke control. Forced lubrication by submerged pump system incorporating a full flow filter. Chrome iron cylinder block fitted with dry type cylinder liners. Special 'straight port' cylinder head of high tensile aluminium alloy featuring hemispherical combustion chambers and twin overhead camshafts operating large valves of 70° included angle. Aluminium alloy pistons. Steel connecting rods fitted with lead indium big end bearings. 2¼ ins. diameter counterweighted crankshaft carried on seven lead indium bearings. Pressurised cooling system with thermostatically controlled, electrically driven twin fans.

TRANSMISSION. Manually operated four speed, single helical all synchromesh gearbox. Ratios : 1st, 9.01 ; 2nd, 5.85 ; 3rd, 4.27 ; 4th, 3.07 ; Reverse, 10.38. Centrally positioned gear change lever. Baulk ring synchromesh on all four forward ratios. Borg & Beck 9½" DS clutch. Hardy Spicer needle bearing propeller shaft. Hypoid rear axle. Ratio 3.07. Differential ratios 3.31 : 1. 3.54. Differential unit mounted in sub-frame carrying the rear suspension. Improvements to helix angles for smoother, quieter running.

SUSPENSION—FRONT. Independent front suspension incorporating transverse wishbones and torsion bars controlled by telescopic hydraulic dampers. Anti-roll bar fitted to lower wishbones.

SUSPENSION—REAR. Fully independent rear suspension incorporating, on each side, a lower transverse tubular link pivoted at the wheel carrier and subframe adjacent to the differential case and above this, a halfshaft universally jointed at each end. These serve to locate the wheel in a transverse plane. Longitudinal location is provided by the rubber mountings locating the sub-assembly in the body structure and by a radius arm between the lower link and a mounting point on the body structure. Twin coil springs, each enclosing a telescopic damper, provide the suspension medium. The whole assembly together with the differential unit is carried in an easily detachable frame which is located in the body structure by rubber mountings.

BRAKES. Disc brakes featuring quick-change pads, are fitted to all four wheels. Front brakes fitted on wheel hubs, rear brakes fitted inboard of half shafts adjacent to differential unit. Suspended vacuum type servo operated by tandem master cylinder. System divided into two entirely independent hydraulic circuits to front and rear brakes. Centrally positioned handbrake operates on rear wheels only. Combined handbrake and brake fluid warning light.

STEERING. Rack and pinion. 16 ins. steering wheel with separate adjustments for height and reach. Number of turns lock to lock 2½. Turning circle 37 ft. diameter. Power-assisted steering available as an optional extra.

WHEELS AND TYRES. Wire spoke wheels with centre lock hubs fitted with Dunlop 185 × 15 tyres and tubes. 'Aquajet' tyre tread. Optional bolt-on chrome-plated pressed-steel wheels available.

FUEL SUPPLY. By S.U. electric pump. Tank of 14 Imperial gallon capacity. Petrol filter incorporated into fuel line and located by engine compartment.

ELECTRICAL EQUIPMENT, INSTRUMENTS AND FITTINGS. Lucas alternator generator. 12-volt negative earth system. Large capacity battery giving 57 amp-hours at 10 hour rate with current voltage control. Eight fuse control box, fully labelled, located behind hinged central facia panel for ease of access. Side lamps. Lucas sealed beam, asymmetric dip, headlamps with hand-operated dipping control on facia. Separate lever actuating headlamp flashing. Separate stop-tail, direction and reflector units mounted in a single assembly. Rear number plate lamps. Twin reversing lights. Flashing direction indicators with self-cancellation and warning light on facia, doubling as hazard warning lights with separate switch on facia. Instruments and labelled switches illuminated by internal floodlighting controlled by a two-position dimmer switch. Map reading light. Interior light. Twin-blended note horns. Triple blade two-speed self-parking windscreen wiper unit. Electrically operated windscreen washers. Cigar lighter with luminous socket. Starter motor. Vacuum and centrifugal automatic ignition control. Oil coil ignition. 5 ins. diameter 160 m.p.h. speedometer incorporating total and trip distance recorders. 5 ins. diameter electrically operated revolution counter. Centrally positioned transistorised clock. Battery condition indicator. Electrically operated water temperature gauge, oil pressure gauge, fuel gauge with low level warning light. Choke warning light. Combined handbrake and brake fluid level warning light. Wiring harness in quickly detachable front body section connected to main circuits through an eight-pin connector mounted on engine compartment bulkhead.

BODY. Stressed shell steel body of patented, monocoque construction. Front sub-frame of square section steel tubing carries engine unit, suspension and forward hinged front section. Two door two seater body of extremely low drag characteristics resulting from intensive wind tunnel testing. The folding hood incorporating a large rear window is of finest quality plastic, mounted on a special frame to permit single handed erection or stowage. When stowed the hood assembly is completely concealed by a separate detachable cover. Fibreglass detachable hardtop available as an optional extra. Counterbalanced, forward opening

front section provides excellent accessibility to all mechanical components. Wrapround windscreen and thin pillars provide superb forward visibility. Door lights completely concealed within doors when fully lowered. Wraparound bumpers with overriders at front and rear. Twin bucket seats, adjustable for reach and rake, upholstered in finest quality Vaumol leather over Dunlopillo foam rubber cushions. Facia and screen rail in matt grained finish to eliminate reflection. Comprehensive instrumentation with revolution counter and speedometer positioned in front of driver. Central panel contains separate fuel gauge and battery condition indicator, together with a row of labelled rocker switches controlling ancillary equipment. Separate housing beneath panel contains a radio and twin speakers (optional extra). When no radio is fitted, the speaker grilles are retained and the radio control panel aperture is blanked off with an escutcheon. Panel in front of passenger contains a lockable glove compartment and grab handle. Three-spoke, alloy, lightweight steering wheel with wood rim. Wide angle rear view mirror in snap-off mounting. Deep pile carpets over thick felt underlay. Luggage accommodation provided in tail of car. Luggage boot lid controlled from inside the car. Seat belt anchorages are incorporated.

HEATING AND DEMISTING. High output fresh air heating and multi-point windscreen demisting system incorporating a two-speed fan controlled by switch on facia. Temperature and volume of air to windscreen and car interior regulated by controls mounted on facia panel. Ducts direct air to each side of compartment.

SPARE WHEEL AND TOOLS. The spare wheel is carried beneath the boot floor in a separate compartment and is readily accessible. The tools, in a roll are housed in the spare wheel compartment.

JACKING. Centrally located jacking sockets enable the front and rear wheels on either side of the car to be raised simultaneously by means of the manually-operated screw type easy lift jack.

PRINCIPAL DIMENSIONS. Wheelbase, 8 ft. 0 ins. Track, front and rear, 4 ft. 2 ins. Overall length, 14 ft. 7¾ ins. Overall width, 5 ft. 5¼ ins. Overall height, 4 ft. 0 ins. Ground clearance (laden) 5½ ins. Dry weight 2790 lbs.

2 + 2 MODEL

PRINCIPAL DIMENSIONS: Wheelbase, 8 ft. 9 ins.; Track, front and rear, 4 ft. 2 ins.; Overall length, 15 ft. 4½ ins.; Overall width, 5 ft. 5¼ ins.; Overall height, 4 ft. 2 ins.; Ground clearance (laden), 5½ ins.; Turning circle, 41 ft.; Fuel tank capacity 14 imp. gallons.

Everything that the **XK-E** had sounded quite alluring. And yet— there were recalls at that time. It was not a happy time for automobile manufacturing in England. Jaguar experienced quality fluctuations too.

INTERIOR DETAIL:

● All switches on instrument panel are of the smooth contoured rocker type.

● Recessed choke and heater controls with "push-pull" action and low friction cables.

● Recessed, disc shape ventilation direction controls.

● Padded screen rail.

● Plastic rimmed rear view mirror with snap-away mounting.

● Recessed door handles.

● Slimline window winders with rubber recessed into handles.

● Lockable glove compartment.

● Horn button, headlamp flasher and direction indicator switch incorporated in one lever.

PLUS JAGUAR'S HIGH STANDARDS OF LUXURIOUS INTERIOR APPOINTMENTS.

JAGUAR CARS LTD. COVENTRY ENGLAND

The issue of this catalogue does not constitute an offer. The specifications described in this publication vary for different countries, and Jaguar Cars Ltd. reserve the right to amend specifications without notice.

Printed in England by W. W. Curtis Ltd., Coventry.

10.69

SERIES 2 'E' TYPE FIXED HEAD COUPÉ

ENGINE. 6 cylinder, twin overhead camshaft, 4.2 litre XK Jaguar engine. 92.07 mm. bore, 106 mm. stroke (3.625" by 4.1732"), cubic capacity 4235 c.c. (258.43 cu. in.). Compression ratio 9 : 1 (8 : 1 optional). Power output (9 : 1) 265 b.h.p. at 5400 r.p.m., torque 283 ft./lb. at 4,000 r.p.m. Three S.U. carburetters, Type HD.8 with manual choke control. Forced lubrication by submerged pump system incorporating a full flow filter. Chrome iron cylinder block fitted with dry type cylinder liners. Special 'straight port' cylinder head of high tensile aluminium alloy featuring hemispherical combustion chambers and twin overhead camshafts operating large valves of 70° included angle. Aluminium alloy pistons. Steel connecting rods fitted with lead indium big end bearings. 2¼ ins. diameter counterweighted crankshaft carried on seven large lead indium bearings. Pressurised cooling system with thermostatically controlled, electrically driven twin fans.

TRANSMISSION. Manually operated four speed, single helical all synchromesh gearbox. Ratios : 1st, 9.01 ; 2nd, 5.85 ; 3rd, 4.27 ; 4th, 3.07 ; Reverse, 10.38. Centrally positioned gear change lever. Baulk ring synchromesh on all four forward ratios. Borg & Beck 9½ DS clutch. Hardy Spicer needle bearing propeller shaft. Hypoid rear axle. Ratio 3.07, Optional ratios 3.31 : 1. 3.54. Differential unit mounted in sub-frame carrying the rear suspension. Improvements to helix angles for smoother, quieter running.

SUSPENSION—FRONT. Independent front suspension incorporating transverse wishbones and torsion bars controlled by telescopic hydraulic dampers. Anti-roll bar fitted to lower wishbones.

SUSPENSION—REAR. Fully independent rear suspension incorporating, on each side, a lower transverse tubular link pivoted at the wheel carrier and subframe adjacent to the differential case and above this, a halfshaft universally jointed at each end. These serve to locate the wheel in a transverse plane. Longitudinal location is provided by the rubber mountings locating the sub-assembly in the body structure and by a radius arm between the lower link and a mounting point on the body structure. Twin coil springs, each enclosing a telescopic damper, provide the suspension medium. The whole assembly together with the differential unit is carried in an easily detachable frame which is located in the body structure by rubber mountings.

BRAKES. Disc brakes featuring quick-change pads, are fitted to all four wheels. Front brakes fitted on wheel hubs, rear brakes fitted inboard of half shafts adjacent to differential unit. Suspended vacuum type servo operated by tandem master cylinder. System divided into two entirely independent hydraulic circuits to front and rear brakes. Centrally positioned handbrake operates on rear wheels only. Combined handbrake and brake fluid warning light.

STEERING. Rack and pinion. 16 ins. steering wheel with separate adjustments for height and reach. Number of turns lock to lock 2½. Turning circle 37 ft. diameter. Power-assisted steering available as an optional extra.

WHEELS AND TYRES. Wire spoke wheels with centre lock hubs fitted with Dunlop 185 × 15 tyres and tubes. 'Aquajet' tyre tread. Optional bolt-on chrome-plated pressed-steel wheels available.

FUEL SUPPLY. By S.U. electric pump. Tank of 14 Imperial gallon capacity. Petrol filter incorporated into fuel line and located by engine compartment.

ELECTRICAL EQUIPMENT, INSTRUMENTS AND FITTINGS. Lucas alternator generator. 12-volt negative earth system. Large capacity battery giving 57 amp-hours at 10 hour rate with current voltage control. Eight fuse control box, fully labelled, located behind hinged central facia panel for ease of access. Side lamps. Lucas sealed beam, asymmetric dip, headlamps with hand-operated dipping control on facia. Separate lever actuating headlamp flashing. Separate stop-tail, direction and reflector units mounted in a single assembly. Rear number plate lamps. Twin reversing lights. Flashing direction indicators with self-cancellation and warning light on facia, doubling as hazard warning lights with separate switch on facia. Instruments and labelled switches illuminated by internal floodlighting controlled by a two-position dimmer switch. Map reading light. Interior light. Twin-blended note horns. Triple blade two-speed self-parking windscreen wiper unit. Electrically operated windscreen washers. Cigar lighter with luminous socket. Starter motor. Vacuum and centrifugal automatic ignition control. 5 ins. diameter 160 m.p.h. speedometer incorporating total and trip distance recorders. 5 ins. diameter electrically operated revolution counter. Centrally positioned transistorised clock. Battery condition indicator. Electrically operated water temperature gauge, oil pressure gauge, fuel gauge with low level warning light. Choke warning light. Combined handbrake and brake fluid low level warning light. Wiring harness in quickly detachable front body section connected to main circuits through an eight-pin connector mounted on engine compartment bulkhead.

BODY. Stressed shell steel body of patented, monocoque construction. Front sub-frame of square section steel tubing carries engine unit, suspension and forward hinged front section. Counterbalanced, forward opening front section provides excellent accessibility to all mechanical components. Wraparound windscreen and thin pillars provide superb forward visibility. Door lights completely concealed within doors when fully lowered. Wraparound bumpers with overriders at front and rear. Twin bucket seats, adjustable for reach and rake, upholstered in finest

quality Vaumol leather over Dunlopillo foam rubber cushions. Facia and screen rail in matt grained finish to eliminate reflection. Comprehensive instrumentation with revolution counter and speedometer positioned in front of driver. Central panel contains separate fuel gauge and battery condition indicator, together with a row of labelled rocker switches controlling ancillary equipment. Separate housing beneath panel contains a radio and twin speakers (optional extra). When no radio is fitted, the speaker grilles are retained and the radio control panel aperture is blanked off with an escutcheon. Panel in front of passenger contains a lockable glove compartment and grab handle. Three-spoke, alloy, lightweight steering wheel with wood rim. Wide angle rear view mirror in snap-off mounting. Deep pile carpets over thick felt underlay. Luggage accommodation provided in tail of car. Luggage boot lid controlled from inside the car. Seat belt anchorages are incorporated.

HEATING AND DEMISTING. High output fresh air heating and multi-point windscreen demisting system incorporating a two-speed fan controlled by switch on facia. Temperature and volume of air to windscreen and car interior regulated by controls mounted on facia panel. Ducts direct air to each side of compartment.

SPARE WHEEL AND TOOLS. The spare wheel is carried beneath the boot floor in a separate compartment and is readily accessible. The tools, in a roll, are housed in the spare wheel compartment.

JACKING. Centrally located jacking sockets enable the front and rear wheels on either side of the car to be raised simultaneously by means of the manually-operated screw type easy lift jack.

PRINCIPAL DIMENSIONS. Wheelbase, 8 ft. 0 ins. Track, front and rear, 4 ft. 2 ins. Overall length, 14 ft. 7⁷⁄₁₆ ins. Overall width, 5 ft. 5¼ ins. Overall height, 4 ft. 0 ins. Ground clearance (laden) 5½ ins. Dry weight 2790 lbs.

Two more pages from a 1968 catalog, this one for the British domestic market. All details are recorded precisely.

Title page of a 1969 catalog,
made up in grand style with a
wealth of good photos.

Chromed spoked wheels, cold-eyed
girl in fur and leather—but the XK-
E was not an off-road vehicle.

In North America there are certain features that are indispensable on a sports-luxury car: automatic transmission, air conditioning, power steering and power-boosted disc brakes at all four wheels, with lavish comfort for two and occasional seating for two more. Such are the accoutrements of the latest 2+2 version of the XK-E, with some of its popular options. Also optional on this unique grand tourer are whitewall tires, tinted glass and an electrically heated rear window defroster.

Jaguar's deceptively sleek four-seater is even cleaner in profile this year with a more steeply raked windshield. Nine inches longer in wheelbase than the other XK-E's, the 2+2 Coupe has a fully upholstered rear seat which can also be folded ingeniously forward to extend the luggage platform.

Incomparably equipped for its price, the 2+2 Coupe is entirely updated this year with high, stronger bumpers and a larger front air inlet. Running and signal lights are enlarged for added safety, and more fully protected from minor damage. Other identification points of the new model include the more forward headlamp placement and the adjustable headrests on the genuine leather front bucket seats.

No other car is capable of offering faster or safer transportation for you and your family.

XK-E 2+2

The type designation makes clear that this catalog too was intended for American customers. The formulation "for you and your family" is somewhat exaggerated— for a couple could travel better alone; even children could be carried well in the back only when they were small.

Main dimensions: Wheelbase 105 ins. Track 50 ins. front and rear. Overall length 184¼ ins. Overall width 65¼ ins. Overall height 50 ins. Ground clearance (laden) 5½ ins. Turns lock to lock 2½. Turning circle 41 ft. Fuel capacity 16¾ gal. Oil capacity 9 qts. Water system 19¼ qts. Dry weight 2,744 lbs. Wheels and tires 15-inch wire-spoke, quick-change hub caps. Dunlop "Aquajet" radial ply 185 x 15 tires and tubes.

Body features: Same as Coupe with the addition of a fully upholstered rear seat for two. The back of the rear seat is horizontally split, permitting the upper half to move forward to increase luggage space to maximum length of 52½ ins. Reclining seats with adjustable headrests. Variable-direction ventilation nozzles on panel.

Optional equipment: Fully automatic transmission with dual-drive range and floor selector. Power steering. Chromium plated wire wheels. Whitewall tires. Tinted glass. Electrically heated rear window. Factory air conditioning.

Chassis features: Six-cylinder twin-overhead-camshaft XK engine. Bore and stroke 3.63 x 4.17 ins. Displacement 4235 cc; 258.4 cu. ins. Compression ratio 9 to 1 with hemispherical combustion chambers. 246 bhp at 5500 rpm; 263 lbs.-ft. of torque at 3000 rpm. Twin Zenith-Stromberg carburetors. Duplex air pollution control manifold. Dual exhaust systems. Oil coil ignition. 12-volt electrical system with heavy duty alternator. Hydraulically-operated clutch. Four-speed transmission, fully synchronized, floor shift. Limited slip differential. Stressed-skin all-steel monocoque body, with front and rear attached suspension and engine sub-frames. Independent front suspension by parallel wishbones, with torsion bars, telescopic shock absorbers and anti-roll bar. Independent rear suspension comprises transverse links, radius arms, quadruple coil springs with four concentric shock absorbers. Rack and pinion steering. Girling four-wheel power-assisted disc brakes.

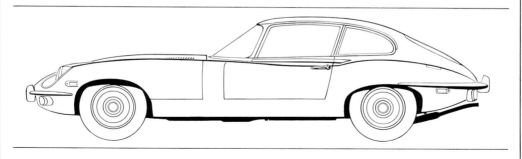

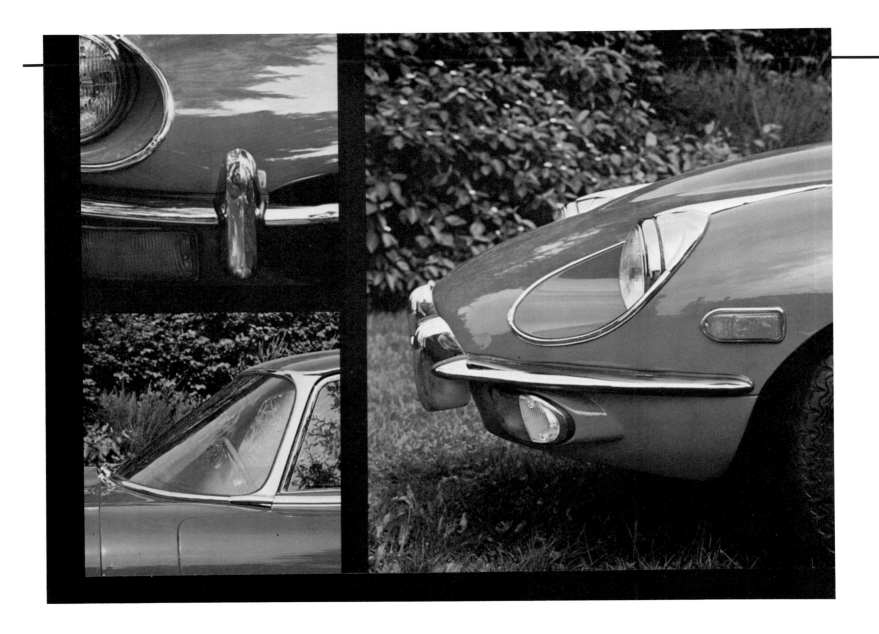

The Jaguar XK-E Roadster is a beautiful two-seater sports car. It is also much more than that. It is five great victories at Le Mans. It is country living in the city. It is Briggs Cunningham, Walt Hansgen and Alfred Momo. It is the sparkle of 72-spoke chromed wire wheels spinning down Wilshire Boulevard. And it is a speedometer that reads to 160 mph because it has to.

Some XK-E Roadster features are classic, unchangeable. Such is the svelte, wind-formed shape, with the louvered hood hinging upward for total access to the aluminum-head twin-camshaft engine, tamed from racing for your enjoyment on the road. And there could be no replacement for the form-fitting reclining seats, the short, stiff lever between them that controls a fully-synchronized four-speed transmission (over 100 miles an hour in third).

Selective improvements in the latest XK-E Roadsters will be applauded by the urbanite: High, bolder bumpers both front and rear, better protection for bright signal lights and wide-spaced exhaust pipes, and a larger front air inlet (an XK-E has no "grille") for maximum cooling when the optional air conditioning is operating in traffic.

Have you ever owned an air-conditioned Jaguar Roadster? Why not this year?

ROADSTER

Main dimensions: Wheelbase 96 ins. Track 50 ins. front and rear. Overall length 175-5/16 ins. Overall width 65¼ ins. Overall height 48 ins. Ground clearance (laden) 5½ ins. Turns lock to lock 2¾. Turning circle 37 ft. Fuel capacity 16¾ gal. Oil capacity 9 qts. Water system 19¼ qts. Dry weight 2,464 lbs. Wheels and tires 15-inch wire-spoke, quick-change hub caps. Dunlop "Aquajet" Radial ply 185 x 15 tires and tubes.

Body features: Quick folding top, fully lined, mounted on a special frame to permit easy raising or lowering. Large rear window. Top concealed when lowered beneath waterproof cover. Access to the luggage compartment in the rear is by an internal key locking release, which raises the deck lid. Additional space for packages is provided behind the reclining seats with adjustable headrests. Lockable glove compartment.

Optional equipment: Lightweight hardtop. Chromium plated wire wheels. Whitewall tires. Tinted glass. Factory air conditioning.

Chassis features: Six-cylinder twin-overhead-camshaft XK engine. Bore and stroke 3.63 x 4.17 ins. Displacement 4,235 cc; 258.4 cu. ins. Compression ratio 9 to 1 with hemispherical combustion chambers. 246 bhp at 5500 rpm; 263 lbs.-ft. of torque at 3000 rpm. Twin Zenith-Stromberg carburetors. Duplex air pollution control manifold. Dual exhaust system. Oil coil ignition. 12-volt electrical system with heavy duty alternator. Hydraulically-operated clutch. Four-speed transmission, fully synchronized, floor shift. Limited slip differential. Stressed-skin all-steel monocoque body, with front and rear attached suspension and engine sub-frames. Independent front suspension by parallel wishbones, with torsion bars, telescopic shock absorbers and anti-roll bar. Independent rear suspension comprises transverse links, radius arms, quadruple coil springs with four concentric shock absorbers. Rack and pinion steering. Girling four-wheel power-assisted disc brakes.

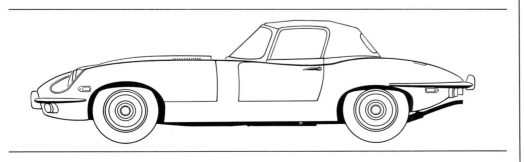

In the USA, roadster and coupe sales were just about equal, while back home in England the closed XK-E was sold more often.

47

Does anyone really need a Jaguar XK-E Coupe? Is there any compelling necessity to own the equivalent of a Gemini capsule for the highway? Many people find they are able to resist the appeal of triple windshield wipers, of a real wood-rimmed aluminum-spoke adjustable steering wheel, of an independent suspension system so supple and precise that the XK-E Coupe becomes an uncanny extension of the driver's senses and desires.

If you cannot resist the XK-E Coupe you'll find it an immensely satisfying and practical automobile. Specially appropriate to this model are the adjustable headrests and new colors, Regency Red and Silver Gray, that are part of the complete XK-E range this year. Factory-fitted air conditioning, a highly-prized Coupe option, operates more efficiently with the larger front air intake of the new XK-E's.

New high, full-width bumpers protect the long nose and the tapered tail, with its wide door offering easy access to the roomy luggage platform. Handsome rocker-type switches, a padded cowl and recessed door handles add luxury while ensuring that the XK-E Coupe, like all Jaguars, meets and exceeds the Federal Safety Standards.

If this kind of personalized motoring appeals to you, you probably already own an XK-E Coupe. How about a new one?

COUPE

Main dimensions: Wheelbase 96 ins. Track 50 ins. front and rear. Overall length 175-5/16 ins. Overall width 65¼ ins. Overall height 48 ins. Ground clearance (laden) 5½ ins. Turns lock to lock 2¾. Turning circle 37 ft. Fuel capacity 16¾ gal. Oil capacity 9 qts. Water system 19¼ qts. Dry weight 2,570 lbs. Wheels and tires 15-inch wire-spoke, quick-change hub caps. Dunlop "Aquajet" radial ply 185 x 15 tires and tubes.

Body features: Large window in rear luggage door, opened by internal release. Rear quarter windows hinged for ventilation. Luggage carried in flat, padded area behind seats, with hinged retainer at front that drops down to increase usable area. Reclining seats with adjustable headrests. Lockable glove compartment. Twin package shelves.

Optional equipment: Chromium plated wire wheels; whitewall tires; tinted glass; electrically heated rear window; factory air conditioning.

Chassis features: Six-cylinder twin-overhead-camshaft XK engine. Bore and stroke 3.63 x 4.17 ins. Displacement 4235 cc; 258.4 cu. ins. Compression ratio 9 to 1 with hemispherical combustion chambers. 246 bhp at 5500 rpm; 263 lbs.-ft of torque at 3000 rpm. Twin Zenith-Stromberg carburetors. Duplex air pollution control manifold. Dual exhaust system. Oil coil ignition. 12-volt electrical system with heavy duty alternator. Hydraulically-operated clutch. Four-speed transmission, fully synchronized, floor shift. Limited slip differential. Stressed-skin all-steel monocoque body, with front and rear attached suspension and engine sub-frames. Independent front suspension by parallel wishbones, with torsion bars, telescopic shock absorbers and anti-roll bar. Independent rear suspension comprises transverse links, radius arms, quadruple coil springs with four concentric shock absorbers. Rack and pinion steering. Girling four-wheel power-assisted disc brakes.

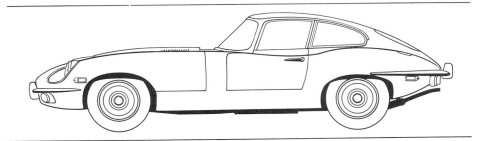

The rear three-quarter view showed off the fastback best. The photo on the opposite page more than does justice to it. "If you are the type for such a car, you probably own one already. How would it be if you bought one again?"— thus the German caption paraphrases the last line on this page.

JAGUAR

Jaguar-Automobile zeichnen sich durch einzigartige Fahreigenschaften aus. Sie sind die Synthese von aussergewöhnlicher Leistung, überragender Strassenhaltung und verlässlicher Bremskraft. Auf der ganzen Welt sind sie das Symbol für wahren Fahrgenuss und höchstes Prestige.

Les Jaguar se distinguent par des qualités routières exceptionnelles, synthèse de la puissance impétueuse du moteur, de la sûreté du freinage, de la tenue de route exemplaire. Partout dans le monde, elles sont le symbole du prestige et du plaisir de conduire.

Limousines: 420 G 265 CV, 420 245 CV, S-Type, 3,8 223 CV, S-Type 3,4 210 CV, 340 213 CV, 240 133 CV, E-Type 265 CV, Coupé, Coupé 2+2, Cabriolet. Preis/prix ab/dès **Fr. 16 350.—** bis/à **Fr. 30 900.—**

Importeur für die deutsche Schweiz: Emil Frey AG, Zürich
Importateur pour la Suisse romande et le Tessin: Garage Place Claparède SA, Genève

Daimler

die älteste englische Automarke
la plus ancienne marque anglaise

V8 250 Saloon 142 CV
4.2 Sovereign Saloon 245 CV
Preis/prix ab/dès **Fr. 21 600.—** bis/à **Fr. 35 700.—**

Daimler-Limousinen werden durch ihre fabelhaften Fahreigenschaften allerhöchsten Ansprüchen gerecht. Die elegante, luxuriöse und sorgfältige Konstruktion zeugt vom Willen der Erbauer, eine ruhmreiche Tradition aufrecht zu erhalten.

Dans les limousines Daimler, l'élégance, le luxe et le soin du détail dénotent la fidélité à une tradition de haut renom. Ces prestigieuses routières satisfont aux plus hautes exigences.

Importateur pour la Suisse: Garage Place Claparède SA, Genève

Jaguar automobiles stand out through unique driving characteristics. They are the synthesis of extraordinary performance, outstanding road-handling and reliable braking power. All over the world they are a symbol of real driving pleasure and highest prestige.
Daimler sedans meet the very highest demands because of their fabulous driving characteristics. The elegant, luxurious and careful construction is born of the manufacturer's desire to maintain a famous tradition.

An advertisement from the catalog of the Automobile Review of the 1968 Geneva Salon.

Jaguar 4.2 XK-E Coupe & Roadster

"A different breed of cat"

Jaguar Cars Inc., 32 East 57th Street, New York, N.Y. 10022

Jaguar XK-E 2+2 Family Coupe
"A DIFFERENT BREED OF CAT"

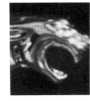

Jaguar
XK-E 2+2 Coupe

Details from a catalog published especially
for the 2 plus 2, portraying the car once
again as a "family coupe." All the details are
described exhaustively in words and pictures.

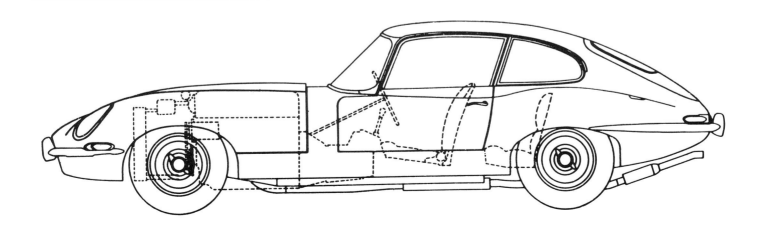

Challenge Jaguar Cars Ltd. of Coventry, England called upon their designers to consider adding two seating places to its 4.2 litre XK-E while retaining the sculptured proportions of this automobile classic. Now, with the introduction of the newest Jaguar — the XK-E 2+2 family coupe — the heritage of the world's most exceptional cars remains intact. Now, the XK-E can be considered by the sportsman who likes his automotive pleasure with one, two or three along . . . family or friends. This dynamic 2+2 fastback maintains the superlative handling qualities of the XK-E and offers unusual spaciousness and cargo area accessibility. The flowing subtlety of the XK-E has been tailored to a new length. By adding 9 inches to the wheelbase and overall length and 2 inches in height, the 2+2 can provide what it promises: 2 extra seats, plus more headroom and legroom for both driver and passengers. Flexible and generous cargo space makes

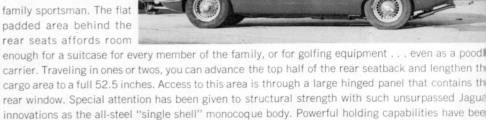

extra sense in a car for the family sportsman. The flat padded area behind the rear seats affords room enough for a suitcase for every member of the family, or for golfing equipment . . . even as a poodle carrier. Traveling in ones or twos, you can advance the top half of the rear seatback and lengthen the cargo area to a full 52.5 inches. Access to this area is through a large hinged panel that contains the rear window. Special attention has been given to structural strength with such unsurpassed Jaguar innovations as the all-steel "single shell" monocoque body. Powerful holding capabilities have been designed into "burst-proof" door catches and locks. But don't let the chromed good looks distract you

The new XK-E 2+2: Jaguar's true family sportscar, available in your choice of 4-speed fully synchromesh gearbox

54

This is the renowned XK engine that tamed Le Mans! Five times in 7 years Jaguar out-powered the best the world had to offer in this, the 24 hour endurance test supreme. This is the engine that will build to 140 mph without any sacrifice in power and mid-speed handling. Power without punishment in a 6-cylinder, 4.2 litre, twin overhead cam engine. And often an extra option on other cars, the XK-E 2 + 2 offers as standard 4-wheel disc brakes with separate systems for front and rear wheels. Now, by the addition of 2 rear seats, the 2 + 2 provides full space for extra passengers. There is sound economy in the luxury of the glove-leather interior as there is in the deep-pile carpet floor covering. Up front are two individually adjustable bucket seats which furnish the cradled-support preferred by

competition drivers the world over. This positive comfort is as important a function of roadability as springs and shocks. Though startlingly like its elder brother in power, the new Jaguar XK-E 2 + 2 model offers safety innovations which will find favor with the Jaguar man who is also a family man. Soft green lights on the instrument panel provide for glareless consultation during nighttime road running. Who thinks about improving glove compartments? Jaguar does. A slight reorientation in the instrument panel has allowed a deeper glove compartment and a wide shelf under the dash for sorting and storing small packages. An emergency warning system which activates all 4 directional signal lights is controlled by a single switch in front of the driver. Improved visibility results from enlarged windshields and 3 extra-length wiper blades. A more effective heating and ventilating system offers greater efficiency in interior heat radiation and cooling. Variable direction outlet nozzles controlled from the dashboard direct air to the area you desire. We suggest that you become familiar with the purring power of this "different breed of cat" by easing yourself behind the wheel of an XK-E 2 + 2 during a visit to our showroom.

agm clutch or the optional dual-drive range automatic transmission.

More pages from the four-page special brochure for the XK-E 2 plus 2.

This catalog of the 1969 models was prepared for the 1968 London Motor Show. Along with all three XK-E variants, it also includes information on the 240 Saloon, the XJ 6 with 2.8 and 4.2 liter motors, and the 420 G. An interesting assortment of models.

Jaguar 'E' Type
series 2
Open Two Seater

ENGINE. Six cylinder 4·2 litre 'XK' engine with twin overhead camshafts and three carburetters. 92·07 mm bore × 106 mm stroke. Capacity 4235 cc, 265 bhp at 5,400 rpm. Compression ratio 9 : 1 (8 : 1 optional). Cross flow radiator, "No loss" cooling system with thermostatically controlled, electrically driven twin fans.

TRANSMISSION. Manually operated four-speed all-synchromesh gearbox. Improved Helix angle for quieter running.

SUSPENSION. (Front) independent suspension—transverse wishbones and torsion bars and telescopic hydraulic dampers. (Rear) fully independent suspension incorporating, on each side, a lower transverse tubular link pivoted at wheel carrier and subframe adjacent to differential case and, above this, a half-shaft universally jointed at each end. Twin coil springs each enclose a telescopic damper.

BRAKES. Servo-assisted disc brakes all round. Independent hydraulic circuits to front and rear brakes.

STEERING. Rack and pinion steering. Collapsible steering column. 2¼ turns lock to lock. Power assisted steering optional extra.

WHEELS AND TYRES. Wire spoke wheels with centre lock hubs. Dunlop SP Sport tyres and tubes. Optional pressed-steel wheels available.

FUEL SUPPLY. 14 Imperial gallon capacity tank. S.U. electric pump.

ELECTRICAL EQUIPMENT AND INSTRUMENTS. Alternator generator. 12-volt battery with negative earth system. Pre-engaged starter motor. Extensive standard equipment includes sealed beam headlamps and headlamp flashing unit, map reading lamp, reversing lamps, flashing direction indicators doubling as hazard warning lights, triple blade two-speed windscreen wipers, windscreen washers, cigar lighter, transistorised clock, automatic ignition advance and comprehensive instrumentation to Jaguar normal high standards.

BODY. Stressed steel two-door two-seater body of monocoque construction. Folding hood with large rear window. (Hard top available as optional extra). Twin semi-reclining bucket seats upholstered in finest quality leather hide over deep Dunlopillo cushions. Deep pile carpets over thick felt underlay.

HEATING AND DEMISTING. High output fresh air heating and multi-point windscreen demisting system. Ducts direct air to each side of car. Two-speed fan.

SPARE WHEEL AND TOOLS. Spare wheel housed beneath boot floor. Comprehensive set of tools. Screw-type easy-lift jack.

PRINCIPAL DIMENSIONS. Wheelbase 8 ft., track front and rear 4 ft. 2 in., overall length 14 ft. 7¾ in., overall width 5 ft. 5¼ in., overall height 4 ft. 0 in., turning circle 37 ft.

More pages from
the 1968 Motor
Show catalog.

Jaguar series 2
'E' Type 2 + 2
Fixed Head Coupé

ENGINE. Six cylinder 4·2 litre 'XK' engine with twin overhead camshafts and three carburetters. 92·07 mm bore × 106 mm stroke. Capacity 4235 cc, 265 bhp at 5,400 rpm. Compression ratio 9 : 1 (8 : 1 optional). Pressurised cooling system with thermostatically controlled twin electric fans.

TRANSMISSION. (Manual) four-speed all-synchromesh gearbox. Centrally positioned gear change lever. (Automatic) Borg Warner Model 8 with dual drive range, D1/D2.

SUSPENSION. (Front) independent by transverse wishbones and torsion bars with telescopic hydraulic dampers. (Rear) fully independent, having, on each side, a lower transverse tubular link pivoted at the rear wheel carrier and subframe adjacent to differential case and, above this, a half-shaft universally jointed at each end. Twin coil springs each enclose a telescopic damper.

BRAKES. Servo-assisted disc brakes all round. Independent hydraulic circuits to front and rear brakes.

STEERING. Rack and pinion steering 2·85 turns lock to lock. Collapsible steering column.

WHEELS AND TYRES. Wire spoke wheels with centre lock hubs. Dunlop SP Sport tyres and tubes. Optional pressed-steel wheels available.

FUEL SUPPLY. 14 Imperial gallons capacity tank. S.U. electric pump.

ELECTRIC EQUIPMENT AND INSTRUMENTS. Alternator, 12-volt battery with negative earth system. Pre-engaged starter motor. Extensive standard equipment includes sealed beam headlamps and head-lamp flashing unit, reversing lamps, map reading lamp, flashing direction indicators doubling as hazard warning lights, cigar lighter, twin-blade two-speed windscreen wiper, windscreen washers, transistorised clock and comprehensive instrumentation to Jaguar normal high standards.

BODY. Two-door, stressed steel monocoque body incorporating four seats fully upholstered in finest quality leather hide over deep Dunlopillo cushions. Top section of rear seat squab moves forward, extending boot floor to give 25% more luggage space when car is used as two-seater. Deep pile carpets over thick underlay.

HEATING AND DEMISTING. High output fresh air heating system gives rapid defrosting and demisting of windscreen. Variable direction nozzles controlled individually by front seat occupants.

SPARE WHEEL AND TOOLS. Spare wheel housed beneath boot floor. Comprehensive set of tools. Screw-type easy-lift jack.

PRINCIPAL DIMENSIONS. Wheelbase 8 ft. 9 in., track front and rear 4 ft. 2 in., overall length 15 ft. 4½ in., overall width 5 ft. 5¼ in., overall height 4 ft. 2 in., turning circle 41 ft.

Right: It can be seen clearly in profile that the windshield of the closed car is at a sharper angle than before—compare with page 30, for example.

Sensational: The Jaguar XK-E with a V-12 motor! In March of 1971 it was introduced at the Geneva Salon, and the car became the very model of the luxurious sports two-seater, blending the greatest comfort with "satiating" performance. The 5.3 liter motor represented the pinnacle of XK-E develop-

ment. The car could be had open or closed, but only with a long wheelbase; the short-chassis version could not be had as a V-12. The production of this uncommon and attractive automobile ended on February 24, 1975.

Port Chester,

First the gate to the world of Jaguars
is closed, then it opens—again, a
photographically charming layout
for a brochure, published in April of
1971.

The Jaguar Convertible.
Several changes have been made in the Convertible enhancing its design. The bumper-brakelight assembly, for example, has been restyled so the lights are now an integral part of the wrap-around bumper. And underneath the bumper is an impressive array of tail-pipes.

The Convertible now measures 15 feet 4 inches in overall length. This adds several extra inches of leg room and trunk room. In addition, doors have been widened to provide for easy entrance and exit.

The newly designed all-weather top can be quickly and easily raised or lowered. It's so snug-fitting you're comfortable even in the most severe weather conditions.

The Jaguar Convertible. The ultimate cat. With a folding top.

The Jaguar 2 + 2.

The 2 + 2, like all Jaguars, takes 8 full weeks to build. It is, of course, a sports car. An enclosed sports car with a host of amenities for touring in the grand style.

The suspension system.

All four wheels are fully independently suspended. A bump on one does not lift another. This isn't mere creature comfort—although it is comfortable—it is creature safety. Moreover, new front-end "anti-dive" geometry, plus torsion bars, has been introduced into the suspension system to make the 2 + 2 sure-footed. And for even surer footing, the track has been appreciably widened.

The steering.

When you turn the wheel, you turn the wheels. No more. No less. The steering is power-assisted rack-and-pinion with 3.5 turns lock-to-lock. And the steering column is adjustable. For extra maneuverability, the turning circle has been reduced from 41 to 36 feet.

The amenities.

The reclining bucket seats are upholstered in top-quality leather of matching color and grain. They fold forward to facilitate entrance and exit to the back seat.

The back seat, in turn, pivots forward to add extra room to the already generous luggage space. A wide-swinging rear door, with an interior release, provides quick and easy access to the luggage compartment.

A most important amenity: a new flow-through ventilation system with an air extractor louver situated on the car's rear panel.

The Jaguar 2 + 2. The ultimate cat. With a permanent roof.

The ultimate cat: inside.
The front bucket seats recline individually and fold forward to facilitate passage to and from the back seat in the 2 + 2 model. Additionally, the back of the rear seat pivots forward to provide the abundant luggage space illustrated on the opposite page. Standard on all models: a retractable, inertia-reel seat-belt system.

Dynamic designs in car and advertising.

The ultimate cat: outside. The ultimate cat has had exterior changes. The fenders are slightly flared. This animal not only claws the road, it also looks like it does. And there's a new unity in the design of the headlamps, parking lights, and turn signals, accentuated by the sweep of the wrap-around bumper. As indicated by the 2 + 2 (below), this animal — even at rest — seems ready to spring.

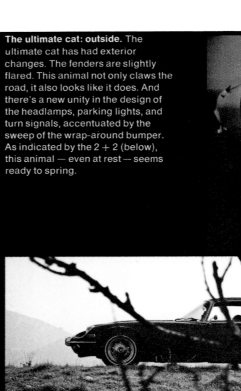

The grille gleams through an oval of chrome. And at its center, the distinguished symbol of Jaguar. Beneath the grille, the new air scoop for more efficient engine ventilation. (Incidentally, eight coats of paint are applied to the body — the last one after the car has been road-tested.)

Jaguar V-12:
The ultimate cat

This is the ultimate cat. Lithe. Sleek. Swift.
Adapted to any motoring environment. With
independent 4-wheel suspension to give this
animal the footing it needs, regardless of
the surface it's running on. With power-
assisted rack-and-pinion steering.
And a new power-assisted braking system
with 10-inch discs in back and new 11-inch
ventilated discs in front. When you want
this cat to stop in its tracks, it stops.

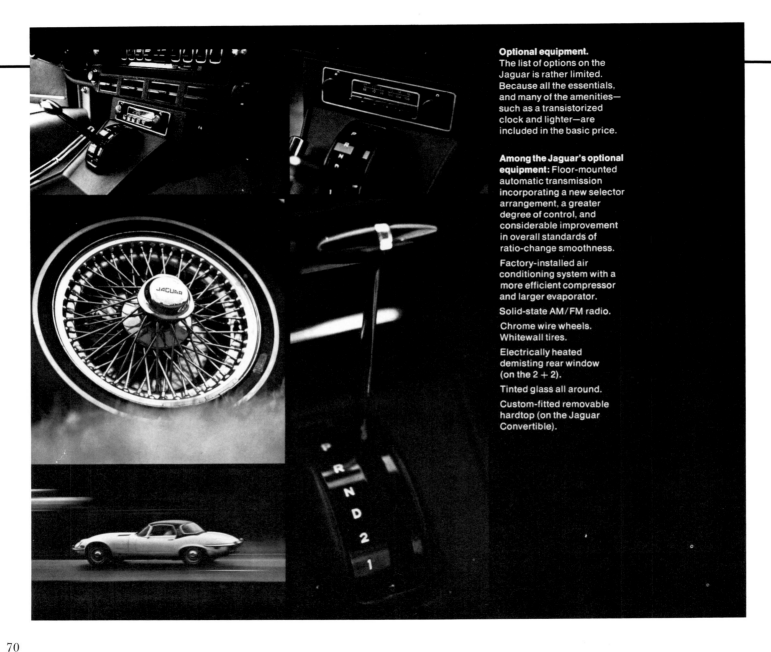

Optional equipment.
The list of options on the
Jaguar is rather limited.
Because all the essentials,
and many of the amenities—
such as a transistorized
clock and lighter—are
included in the basic price.

**Among the Jaguar's optional
equipment:** Floor-mounted
automatic transmission
incorporating a new selector
arrangement, a greater
degree of control, and
considerable improvement
in overall standards of
ratio-change smoothness.

Factory-installed air
conditioning system with a
more efficient compressor
and larger evaporator.

Solid-state AM/FM radio.

Chrome wire wheels.
Whitewall tires.

Electrically heated
demisting rear window
(on the 2 + 2).

Tinted glass all around.

Custom-fitted removable
hardtop (on the Jaguar
Convertible).

JAGUAR V-12 SPECIFICATIONS

ENGINE
12-cylinder water-cooled aluminum 60-degree "V" with overhead camshafts (1 per bank).
3-plane, 7-bearing crankshaft.
Exhaust and evaporative emission control.
Compression ratio: 9:1
Bore: 3.543 in.
Stroke: 2.756 in.
Stroke/bore ratio: 0.779:1
Displacement: 5343 c.c. (326.06 cu. in.)
Horsepower: 314 b.h.p. gross at 6,200 r.p.m.
Torque: 349 lb./ft. gross at 3,800 r.p.m.
Ignition: Opus Mark II Electronic System consisting of electronic distributor with timing rotor, amplifier unit, ballast resistance unit, and special high performance coil.
Carburetion: Four Zenith-Stromberg 175 CD2SE carburetors.
Fuel Pump: 1.5 p.s.i. S.U. electric.
Fuel Tank Capacity: 20.25 U.S. gallons.
Sump Capacity: 11.5 quarts.

TRANSMISSION — Manual:
Four-speed all synchromesh.
Clutch: Diaphragm spring-type Borg & Beck 10.5 in. with hydraulic actuation.
Limited slip differential.
Rear Axle Ratio: 3.54:1.
Overall Gear Ratios: First 10.38:1, Second 6.75:1, Third 4.92:1, Fourth 3.54:1, Reverse 11.95:1.

TRANSMISSION — Automatic (Optional):
Borg Warner three-speed fully automatic with torque converter.
Limited slip differential.
Rear Axle Ratio: 3.31:1.
Overall Gear Ratios:
   1   6.82 — 13.24
   2   4.8 — 9.6
   Drive: 6.62:1 with torque conversion.

STEERING:
Rack-and-pinion, power assisted. Adjustable steering column.
Steering Ratio: 18:1.
Turns lock to lock: 3.5.
Turning Circle: 36 feet.

SUSPENSION:
Front: Independent transverse wishbones with torsion bars, monotube hydraulic shock absorbers, and anti-roll bar. Incorporates "anti-dive" geometry.
Rear: Wishbones with drive shaft forming upper link, radius arms, monotube hydraulic shock absorbers inside coil springs, and anti-roll bar.

BRAKES:
Power-assisted 4-wheel disc brakes.
Front: 11.18 in. diameter ventilated discs.
Rear: inboard 10.38 in. diameter solid discs.

ROAD WHEELS:
Ventilated pressed steel, 15 in. diameter fitted with Dunlop E70VR 15 SP sport radial-ply tires.

PERFORMANCE DATA:
Maximum Speed: 135+ m.p.h.
Acceleration: 0-60 m.p.h. — 6.8 sec.
Standing Quarter Mile: 14.8 sec.
Road Speed at 1,000 r.p.m. in top gear:
   Manual gearbox: 21.4 m.p.h.
   Automatic: 22.9 m.p.h.

ELECTRICAL:
Negative ground, 12-volt system.
Battery rating: 60 amps at 20 hours.
Alternator: 60 amps.

INSTRUMENTS:
Speedometer with trip odometer.
Electric tachometer.
Battery indicator, oil pressure, water temperature, and fuel gauges.
Clock.
Manual choke.
High-pressure electrically operated windshield washer.
Brake fluid/handbrake, oil pressure, direction indicator, emergency flasher, and choke-control warning lights.
Door-operated courtesy and map-reading lights.
All instruments and switches set in no-glare, padded dash.

BODY:
All-steel monocoque construction with separate engine sub-frame.
Convertible: 2 passenger. Quick-folding top.
2+2: 2-4 passenger with fully upholstered rear seat; rear seat pivots forward to increase luggage compartment area to maximum length of 52.5 inches.

INTERIOR:
Semi-reclining bucket seats leather-faced with ambla panels on non-wearing surfaces.
Inertia-reel seat belts.
Cigarette lighter and ashtray.
Lockable glove box and console.
Ambla-trimmed interior.
Fitted carpet with rubber inserts.

OPTIONAL EQUIPMENT:
Automatic transmission.
Factory-installed air conditioning.
Solid-state AM/FM pushbutton radio.
Whitewall radial-ply tires.
Chrome wire wheels (requires tubed tires).
Tinted glass.
Electrically heated rear window (2+2 only).
Removable hardtop (Convertible only).

JAGUAR CARS CONFORM TO U.S. FEDERAL MOTOR VEHICLE SAFETY AND AIR POLLUTION STANDARDS APPLICABLE AT THEIR DATE OF MANUFACTURE.
SPECIFICATIONS AND COLORS SUBJECT TO CHANGE WITHOUT NOTICE.

BRITISH LEYLAND MOTORS INC.,
LEONIA, NEW JERSEY 07605

MAIN DIMENSIONS:
Overall length: 184.38 in.
Overall height: Convertible, 48.13 in. 2 + 2, 51.13 in.
Overall width: 66.06 in.
Wheelbase: 105 in.
Track at Front: 54.38 in.
Track at Rear: 53.75 in.
Ground Clearance (minimum): 5.38 in.
Weight: 3435 lbs.
Trunk Capacity: Convertible—4.75 cu. ft.
                  2 + 2—9.5 cu. ft.-12.5 cu. ft.

BODY COLORS:

ASCOT FAWN   BLACK   BRITISH RACING GREEN

DARK BLUE   LIGHT BLUE   OLD ENGLISH WHITE

PALE PRIMROSE   SABLE   SIGNAL RED

SILVER GREY   REGENCY RED   WILLOW GREEN

COLOR COORDINATED INTERIOR TRIM AVAILABLE.

SERIES 3 E-TYPE

JAGUAR

Another catalog for the Jaguar XK-E V-12, published in March of 1971. It is a rarity, like the car it portrays.

The series of photos
describes a trip to Italy.
Excellent pictures full
of atmosphere.

73

A collection of pictures from
a photo safari with an **XK-E**,
in a color brochure with
pizzazz. Loads of atmosphere
here . . .

A look into the engine compartment of the Series 3 XK-E. Here pictures could be taken easily—after all, the front hood opened far enough to let everything be seen. As accessible as in a racing car.

Ever since its very first appearance, the Jaguar E-Type has been instantly identifiable, all over the world, by its distinctive and highly individual styling and has become one of Britain's most successful exports.

Now, in Series Three form, it enters a new and even more exciting phase of its career. With many important advancements in design, and with the new Jaguar V12 engine as the principal feature, it continues to be one of the world's most desirable cars.

The small print: advice that is seldom seen so explicitly in a car catalog . . .

SPECIFICATIONS

12-CYLINDER FOUR-STROKE MOTOR, bore 90 mm, stroke 80 mm, displacement 5343 cc, maximum power 314 HP at 6200 rpm, DIN HP 272 at 5850 rpm, maximum torque 48.25 mkg at 3800 rpm, DIN 42.03 mkg at 3600 rpm. highest operating pressure 10.62 kg/cc at 3600 rpm. DIN 9.91 kg/cc at 3600 rpm. Compression 9:1. Single overhead camshaft per cylinder head. Four Zenith Stromberg carburetors. Lucas Opus Mark 2 transistor ignition. Radiator with vertical airflow, with thermostatically controlled, electrically operated fan.

4.2 LITER MOTOR, in-line six-cylinder motor, two overhead camshafts, two carburetors. Bore 92.07 mm, stroke 106 mm, displacement 4235 cc. Maximum power 187 HP at 5000 rpm, DIN 171 HP at 4500 rpm. Maximum torque 32.8 mkg at 3000 rpm, DIN 31.8 mkg at 2500 rpm.

GEARBOX, either fully synchronized 4-speed gearbox or Borg-Warner Model 12 automatic transmission (P, R, N, D, 2, 1).

SUSPENSION, independent suspension of all four wheels, with front anti-dive geometry.

BRAKES, disc brakes with servo power on all wheels, front air-cooled, two-cycle brake system.

STEERING, rack-and-pinion steering with servo power. Energy-absorbing construction of the steering column offers collision protection. Leather steering wheel.

WHEELS, wide painted steel wheels with chromed hubcaps. Dunlop SP Sport belted tires, size EV 70 VR 15. Chromed steel wheels or spoked wheels available optionally.

FUEL SYSTEM, electric fuel pump, 82-liter tank.

ELECTRICAL EQUIPMENT AND INSTRUMENTS, DC generator, 12-volt battery with negative grounding, starter, light system with warning light. Instruments include oil pressure gauge, water thermometer, battery charge indicator, twin windshield wipers with two speeds, windshield washing system with two ducts, effective also at high speeds.

BODY, self-bearing body, bolted-on subframe for motor and front suspension, your choice of two-seat convertible (hardtop at extra cost) or 2+2 coupe. Seats with adjustable backs.

HEATING AND COOLING, high-performance fresh-air heating system with 'through-flow' defroster ducting in the 2+2 coupe and hardtop models.

MEASUREMENTS, overall length 468.4 cm, width 167.8 cm, wheelbase 266.7 cm, front track 138.7 cm, rear track 134.6 cm, turning circle 11 meters.

SPECIFICATIONS SOMMAIRES

MOTEUR V12 Douze cylindres Vé de 60°, 5,3 litres. Alésage 90mm x course 70mm. Cylindrée 5343cm³. Puissance maxi au frein BRUTE: 314 à 6200 tr/mn. DIN: 272 à 5850 tr/mn. Couple maxi BRUTE: 48,25 mkg à 3800 tr/mn. DIN 42,03 kgm à 3600 tr/mn. PMEF maxi BRUTE: 10,62 kg/cm² à 3600 tr/mn. DIN: 9,91 kg/cm² à 3600 tr/mn.
Taux de compression 9:1. Un seul arbre à cames en tête par rangée. Quatre carburateurs Zenith-Stromberg. Allumage électronique Lucas Opus Mark 2. Radiateur à écoulement vertical avec ventilateurs électriques commandés par thermostat.

MOTEUR 4,2 LITRES 6 cylindres en ligne; double arbres à cames; deux carburateurs. 92,07 mm d'alésage x 106 mm de course. Cylindrée 4235 cc. Puissance maxi au frein BRUTE 187 à 5000 tr/mn; DIN 171 à 4500 tr/mn. Couple maxi BRUTE 32,8 kgm à 3000 t/min; DIN 31,8 kgm à 2500 t/min.

TRANSMISSION Choix de boîte de vitesse manuelle à quatre vitesses toutes synchronisées ou transmission automatique Borg Warner Modèle 12 (P,R,N,D,2,1).

SUSPENSION Suspension indépendante sur les quatre roues, comportant une géométrie 'anti-piquage' à l'avant.

FREINS Freins à disque assistés sur les quatre roues. Type à aération à l'avant. Double circuit de liquide pour plus de sécurité.

DIRECTION De type à crémaillère et assistée. Colonnes de direction supérieure et inférieure télescopiques. Volant concave avec jante garnie de cuir.

ROUES ET PNEUS Roues à jante large, en acier embouti, peintes, avec enjoliveurs de jante chromés. Pneus Dunlop Sport SP radiaux EV70VR15. Roues en acier embouti chromé et roues à rayons chromées en supplément en option.

ESSENCE Réservoir de 82 litres. Pompe électrique.

APPAREILS ELECTRIQUES ET INSTRUMENTATION Alternateur. Batterie 12 volts. Masse négative. Démarreur pré-engagé. L'éclairage comporte un système de signalisation de danger. Les instruments comportent un manomètre de pression de l'huile et l'indication de la temperature de l'eau et de l'état de la batterie. Essuie-glaces jumelés à deux vitesses. Lave-glace ultra rapide à double jet.

CARROSSERIE Section principale monocoque. Soubassement boulonné pour le moteur et la suspension avant. Choix entre voiture découverte 2 places (hardtop en supplément en option) et coupé non décapotable 2+2. Sièges à demi inclinables pour les deux modèles.

CHAUFFAGE ET DESEMBUAGE Système de chauffage et désembuage de haut rendement avec renouvellement de l'air et ventilation "through-flow" sur les modèles 2+2 et à hardtop en option.

COTES PRINCIPALES Longeur hors-tout 4,684 m. Largeur hors-tout 1,678 m. Empattement 2,667 m. Voie avant 1,387 m. Voie arrière 1,346 m. Rayon de braquage 5,5 m.

RIASSUNTO DELLE CARATTERISTICHE

MOTORE V12 Dodeci cilindri a V a 60°; diametro e corsa mm. 90 x 70; cilindrata totale 5343 cc Potenza massima lorda 314 HP a 6200 g/m. DIN: 272 HP a 5850 g/m. Coppia massima lorda 48,25 kgm a 3800 g/m. DIN: 42,03 kgm a 3600 g/m.
Pressione media effettiva al freno lorda: 10,6 kg/cmq. a 3600 g/m. DIN: 9,9 kg/cmq a 3600 g/m.
Rapporto di compressione 9:1 Un solo albero distribuzione in testa per linea.
Quattro carburatori Zenith-Stromberg. Accensione elettronica Lucas Opus Mark 2. Radiatore a flusso verticale, con ventilatore a comando termostatico.

MOTORE 4,2 6 cilindri in linea; due alberi di distribuzione; due carburatori. Diametro dei cilindri 92,07 mm. Corsa mm 106. Cilindrata totale 4235 cm³. Potenza massima lorda 187 CV a 5000 giri/min; DIN 171 a 4500 giri/min. Coppia massima lorda 32,8 kgm a 3000 giri/min; DIN 31,8 kgm a 2500 g/m.

TRASMISSIONE Cambio manuale a quattro rapporti sincronizzati oppure cambio automatico Borg Warner modello 12 (P,R,N,D,2,1).

SOSPENSIONE a ruote indipendenti, con geometria a prova di impennata, sulle sospensioni anteriori

FRENI a disco, servoassistiti, sulle quattro ruote, con ventilazione sui freni anteriori. Doppio circuito frenante, per accentuare la sicurezza.

STERZO a cremagliera, servoassistito. Due snodi che arretrano, in caso d'urto. Volante concavo con corona foderata di pelle.

RUOTE E PNEUMATICI Ruote di acciaio stampato, con cerchioni grandi dotati di motivi decorativi. Pneumatici radiali Dunlop SP Sport EV70VR15. Ruote in acciaio stampato cromato, con raggi, a richiesta.

SERBATOIO DEL CARBURANTE di litri 82 con pompa elettrica di alimentazione.

IMPIANTO ELETTRICO E STRUMENTI Alternatore. Batteria di 12V. Impianto con negativo a massa. Motorino di avviamento a preinnesto. Empianto di illuminazione con avvisatori di pericolo. Manometro dell'olio, termometro dell'agua ed indicatore carica della batteria. Tergicristallo a due racchette, a due velocità; lavacristallo a due getti.

CARROZZERIA Scocca autoportante. Telaietto supplementare imbullonato per il motore e sospensioni anteriori. Nella versione aperta a 2 posti (tetto rigido a richiesta) e coupé 2 + 2. Sedili semireclinabili per entrambe le versioni.

RISCALDAMENTO E VENTILAZIONE Sistema di riscaldamento e deappanamento con rinnovo continuo dell'aria sulle versioni 2 + 2 e a tetto rigido.

DIMENSIONI PRINCIPALI Lunghezza complessiva metri 4,684. Larghezza metri 1,678. Passo metri 2,667. Carregiata anteriore metri 1,387. Carregiata posteriore metri 1,346. Diametro di sterzata, metri 11.

SPEZIFIKATION

12-ZYLINDER-VIERTAKT-V-MOTOR Bohrung: 90 mm. Hub: 80 mm. Hubraum: 5343 ccm. Höchstleistung: 314 bei 6200 U/min.; DIN-PS 272 bei 5850 U/min. Höchstdrehmoment: 48,25 mkg bei 3800 U/min.; DIN: 42,03 mkg bei 3600 U/min. Höchstbetriebsdruck: 10,62 kg/cm² bei 3600 U/min.; DIN: 9,91 kg/cm² bei 3600 U/min. Verdichtung: 9:1 Eine obenliegende Nockenwelle pro Zylinderkopf. Vier Zenith-Stromberg-Vergaser, Lucas Opus Mark 2 Transistorzündung, Kühlerblock mit Senkrechtdurchfluss mit Thermostat gesteuertem, elektrisch angetriebenem Ventilator.

4,2 LITER-MOTOR Sechszylinder-Reihenmotor; zwei obenliegenden Nockenwellen; zwei Vergasern. Bohrung 92,07 mm. Hub 106 mm. Hubvolumen 4235 ccm. Höchstleistung 187 bei 5000 U/min; DIN-PS 171 bei 4500 U/min. Höchstdrehmoment 32,8 kgm bei 3000 U/min; DIN 31,8 bei 2500 U/min.

GETRIEBE Entweder vollsynchronisiertes 4-Gang—Getriebe oder Borg Warner Getriebeautomatik Modell 12 (P,R,N,D,2,1).

RADAUFHÄNGUNG Unabhängige Radaufhängung aller vier Räder, vorn mit Anti-Dive—Geometrie.

BREMSEN Scheibenbremsen mit Servounterstutzung an allen Rädern, vorn belüftet. Zweikreisbremssystem.

LENKUNG Zahnstangenlenkung mit Servounterstützung. Energie-absorbierende Konstruktion der Lenksäule bietet Aufprallschutz. Lederlenkrad.

RÄDER Briete, lackierte Stahlfelge mit verchromter Radkappe. Dunlop SP-Sport-Gurtelreifen EV70VR15. Auf Wunsch verchromte Stahlfelge oder verchromtes Speichenrad erhältlich.

KRAFTSTOFFSYSTEM Elektrische Benzinpumpe, 82-Liter-Tank.

ELEKTRISCHE AUSSTATTUNG UND INSTRUMENTE Drehstromlichtmaschine, 12 Volt Batterie mit Minuserde, voreingerückter Anlasser, Beleuchtungsanlage mit Warnlicht. Die Instrumente umfassen Öldruckmesser, Kühlwassertemperaturmesser sowie Batterieladeanzeige. Zwillingsscheibenwischer mit zwei Geschwindigkeiten. Scheibenwaschanlage mit zwei Dusen, wirksam auch bei hohen Geschwindigkeiten.

KAROSSERIE selbsttragende Karosserie, verschrauber Hilfsrahmen für Motor- und Vorderradaufhängung. Wahlweise zweisitziges Kabriolett (Hardtop mit Mehrpreis) und 2+2 Coupé. Sitze mit tief verstellbarer Rückenlehne.

HEIZUNG UND ENTFROSTUNG Leistungsstarkes Frischluftheizsystem mit Entfroster. "Through-flow" Belüftung beim 2+2 Coupé und bei Hardtop-Modellen.

ABMESSUNGEN Gesamtlänge 468,4 cm; Gesamtbreite 167,8 cm; Radstand 266,7 cm; Spurweite vorn 138,7 cm; Spurweite hinten 134,6 cm Wendekreis 11 m.

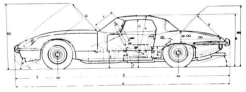

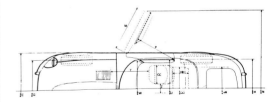

Specification table in four languages—besides listing details in English, this sheet also has them in French, Italian and German.

THE E-TYPE WITH A DIFFERENCE

DIMENSIONS — FIXED HEAD COUPÉ

		Ins.	Cms.
A	Overall length	184.4	468.4
B	Overall height	51.4	130.6
C	Overall width	66.1	167.8
D	Wheelbase	105.0	266.7
E	Front overhang	36.3	92.0
F	Rear overhang	43.13	109.5
G	Front track	54.25	138.0
H	Rear track	53.25	135.3
J	Ground clearance — unladen	5.9	15.0
	— laden	5.4	13.7
K	Front clearance angle	21°	
L	Rear clearance angle	15°	
M	Door opening width	40.5	102.9
N	Overall width doors open	134.0	340.4
O	Ground to top of door	46.5	118.1
P	Door open aperture	35.0	88.9
Q	Bonnet aperture	33.7	85.7
R	Rear door aperture	28.0	71.1
S	Door step height	16.0	40.6
T	Windscreen depth	28.25	71.7
U	Shoulder room	49.0	124.5
V	Front headroom	35.5	90.2
W	Windscreen width (mean)	49.0	124.5
X	Pedals to cushion	19.75	50.2
Y	Front bulkhead to seat cushion	28.5	72.87
Z	Width between seats	9.0	22.9
AA	Front seat height	10.25	26.0
BB	Front seat depth	18.5	47.0
CC	Front seat width	17.8	45.3
DD	Rear headroom	33.0	83.8
EE	Rear seat height	10.0	25.4
FF	Rear seat depth	14.0	35.6
GG	Height of rear seat squab	17.0	43.2
HH	Width of rear seat squab (Min)	39.0	99.1
JJ	Steering wheel to cushion	8.6	21.9
KK	Steering wheel to seat squab	20	50.8
LL	Steering wheel reach adjustment	15	38.1
MM	Steering wheel diameter	2.75	5.7
NN	Rear knee room	7.5	19.1
OO	Maximum boot width	39.0	99.1
PP	Minimum boot width	36.0	91.4
QQ	Maximum boot length	52.5	133.4
RR	Minimum boot length	42.0	106.7
SS	Boot capacity	8-11 cu.ft.	0.22-0.31 cu.m.
TT	Maximum height boot open	72.5	184.1
UU	Maximum height bonnet open	58.3	148.0

DIMENSIONS — ROADSTER

		Ins.	Cms.
A	Overall length	184.4	468.4
B	Overall height	48.4	122.6
C	Overall width	66.1	167.8
D	Wheelbase	105.0	266.7
E	Front overhang	36.3	92.0
F	Rear overhang	43.1	109.5
G	Front track	54.25	138.0
H	Rear track	53.25	135.3
J	Ground clearance — unladen	5.9	15.0
	— laden	5.4	13.7
K	Front clearance angle	21°	
L	Rear clearance angle	15°	
M	Door opening width	40.5	102.9
N	Overall width doors open	134.0	310.4
O	Ground to top of door	43.0	109.2
P	Door open aperture	35.0	88.9
Q	Bonnet open aperture	33.7	85.7
R	Boot open aperture	29	73.7
S	Door step height	16	40.6
T	Windscreen depth	19.2	48.8
U	Shoulder room	49.5	125.8
V	Headroom	33.0	83.8
W	Windscreen width (mean)	50.0	127.0
X	Pedals to cushion	22.3	56.5
Y	Front bulkhead to seat cushion	31.8	82.0
Z	Width between seats	9.0	22.9
AA	Seat height	11.0	27.9
BB	Seat depth	18.5	47.0
CC	Seat width	17.8	45.3
DD	Seat back to rear bulkhead	15.8	40.0
EE	Rear parcel box height	21.5	31.8
FF	Maximum rear parcel box depth	8	20.3
GG	Rear parcel box length	38.3	97.1
HH	Rear parcel box width	15.5	39.4
JJ	Steering wheel to seat cushion	8.6	21.9
KK	Steering wheel to seat squab	22.8	57.8
LL	Steering wheel reach adjustment	2.8	5.7
MM	Steering wheel diameter	15.0	38.1
NN	Maximum boot width	39.0	99.1
OO	Maximum boot length	41.0	104.1
PP	Maximum boot depth	10.3	25.0
QQ	Cubic capacity of boot	4.75 cu.ft.	0.133 cu.m.
RR	Maximum height boot open	56.1	142.7
SS	Maximum height bonnet open	58.3	148.0

All measurements are for an unladen car with seats in mid position total travel 5.75 ins. (14.61 cms.) with a 1 in. (2.5 cm.) rise.

N.B.: WEIGHT CONDITIONS:— Unladen — car with petrol on the road
Laden — car with petrol on the road with four persons and luggage.

The Jaguar V-12 engine. The objective of Jaguar, in its engineering of the V-12 engine, was smoothness of engine performance. Not brute power □ Because of its inherent balance, the engine idles in near silence with virtually no vibration. It powers the Jaguar to 60 m.p.h. in 6.8 seconds with such sinuous grace that one hardly experiences a sensation of motion. And even at full 6500 rpm there is an eerie absence of engine noise □ Of significance is its power to displacement ratio. Jaguar's V-12 displaces only 326 cubic inches and develops 258 SAE horsepower □ Of additional significance is its power-to-engine weight ratio. The total engine weight: an unexpected 680 pounds. Reason: the Jaguar V-12 engine is almost all aluminum □ The V-12's flat head design (with a single camshaft per bank as a natural corollary) was chosen only after tests with various designs plus previous experience gained with Coventry Climax racing engines. The V-12's flat head design produces excellent torque throughout the lower and middle speed ranges. This is especially useful in today's city-to-thruway kind of driving □ The bore/stroke measurements are also rather unusual—a 3½-inch bore and a 2¾-inch stroke. This means the cylinder is unusually wide and the piston stroke unusually short. The advantage: it provides lower piston speed for longer engine life □ Another revolutionary development: a transistorized ignition system. This system, race-proven in Formula 1 cars, employs a new electronic distributor that eliminates all contact points. With no contact points to wear or foul, a major cause of engine tune-ups is eliminated. (Incidentally, an out-of-tune engine is a major cause of engine pollution.) □ Every single V-12 engine—not just an occasional one—is thoroughly and exhaustively tested. Besides individual testing of components, each engine with its clutch and gearbox is bench-tested as a unit—not once but several times. (Final engine approval, of course, is reserved until 2 different road tests by 2 different crews.) □ This then is Jaguar's latest contribution to automotive history: the new V-12. In our opinion, it is the finest production engine in any automobile regardless of size, regardless of price

Left: The XK-E was rarely seen with its hardtop on. It was made of plastic and looked fine on the roadster.

Above: It was a relative of the XK-E but remained only a prototype—the XJ 13 as a racing two-seater, capable of road use and with the typical 'big cat' image.

The motoring press picked up the XK-E even before its official debut—prominent journalists, at least in England, were provided with pre-production test cars, on which reports appeared in print while the 1961 Geneva Salon was going on, in such journals as *The Autocar* and *The Motor*. The international press got on the trail at once and followed up the story; the Americans in particular were especially zealous—after all, the XK-E was a sports car that was designed mainly for sale in the USA.

Motor Trend, Car and Driver, Sports Cars Illustrated—they were all excited about the new Jaguar. Reports followed from Switzerland, Germany, France and Holland.

"It is an old ideal of auto constructors to build a car that unites the characteristics of a racing car and a touring sedan. Since these contradict each other at certain points, the goal remains unattainable. No one has come closer to it—at a reasonable price, at least—than Sir William Lyons with his Jaguar "XK-E.""

This introduction to a test report in the journal *Automobil, Technik-Sport-Touristik*, from the year the Jaguar XK-E appeared, expressed clearly that this sports car ranked among the most fascinating means of propulsion that had ever been made available to the testing department. An XK-E roadster, just as it was tested, the cost 26,000 Marks, which was a lot of money, of course, but still well below the prices of comparable German or Italian super-sports cars.

"If you say the Jaguar 'E' is the fastest actual production car in the world at this time, that is simply not enough. There are, of course, very few cars that reach an everyday top speed of 240 kph and can be bought for a reasonable price, and yet this writer finds this fact alone insufficient to express

what the Jaguar 'E' really is: a true high point in automobile construction."

None of the test cars that had been tested at that time had shown such overwhelming performance along with such great driving safety. With a power-to-weight ratio of only 4.5 kg/HP (on paper), one could be sure of one thing: "This is a value that is hitherto unknown among production cars. In spite of that, this car is nothing like a dangerous thunderbolt that only experienced athletes can enjoy without danger. Quite the opposite: its steering is feather-light and absolutely precise, it is remarkably comfortably sprung for a fast car, and the big six-cylinder motor is quite unexpectedly good-natured."

The tester was very much impressed by the ease with which the XK-E unleashed its great power:

"The top speed that most middle-class cars are capable of is reached by the Jaguar 'E' in second gear, and when you are rolling along the superhighway in fourth gear at 100 kph and step on the gas pedal just once, you reach 160 kph in barely 12 seconds. The speedometer needle goes from 100 to 200 kph in about the same time that it takes a "normal car" to accelerate from 80 to 120 kph. And all this takes place without noise, without vibration, without opposition from the steering wheel and without any wind noise worth mentioning."

But after this opening paean of praise there came a teardrop. It did not appear to be a pleasure for everyone to sit in the XK-E.:

"The biggest failing of the Jaguar 'E': only people of no more than medium height sit comfortably. Whoever has been blessed by fate with long legs will have a hard time settling in. Even the adjustable-length steering column does not help much!

"The foot space is narrow, even too small for men's size 8 shoes, and with a floor that is set at a thoroughly nonsensical angle . . ."

Other failings of the original XK-E included a lack of practical storage space for the indispensable small items that one habitually carries in a car. The tester had his own experience with the open glove compartment: "It is completely useless when the car is driven with its top down. On one of our measured trips, we left a pencil in it: at 170 kph it rattled around, then rose up in the air and sailed away, never to be seen again."

Tester Olaf von Fersen found the old-fashioned gearbox that the Series 1 driver had to mess with even worse than a cramped cockpit: "The four-speed transmission with which all Jaguar cars are delivered today would be better off in a three-ton truck than a sports car. To be sure, it is robust, and its short stick shift fits the hand nicely, but it requires much too much strength. The synchronizing—only for second to fourth gears— can no longer live up to modern concepts. If one drives even a little bit fast, then one has to give gas in between while shifting down and double-clutch when shifting up if one doesn't want to endure long shifting pauses."

Before the tester gave more attention to the operation of the convertible top, he could not avoid mentioning that the XK-E was also available as a picture-pretty coupe: "It looks like a woman with ideal measurements wearing a skin-tight evening gown— . . . quite improperly beautiful!"

When the weather allowed top-down driving, opening the top was no problem: "Opening and closing the top is child's play. The top disappears into its well behind the seat backs (taking up the little space left inside the bodywork for luggage). A cover that goes on with no trouble closes the well neatly and prevents the material from flapping at high speeds. Then we drove down the superhighway

at a good deal over 200 kph. Of course there is a bit of a breeze, but it is not at all unpleasant or overly sporting."

All in all, driving this 265-HP car was quite unspectacular once one had gotten used to the length of the front end as seen from behind the overlong motor hood:

"The motor always starts immediately but needs to run for a few seconds before it is willing to work. After driving about one kilometer, the water thermometer rises to its usual range and the choke is no longer needed."

"The XK-E's disc brakes were rated highly, as they meant there was no danger in driving the car at high speeds: "They are the "safest" brakes we have ever met. One can apply their full power—if needed—at 200 kph without concern, and without the car going

The big cat shows its teeth:
Jaguar XK-E Series 3 of 1971-75.

Right: Dashboard of a Series 2 XK-E (1968-71); on the opposite page is the cockpit of an early Series 1 car.

the least bit off its course or even becoming uneasy! The hand brake is scarcely more than a dummy that only serves to hold the car on a modest slope."

The test car's average fuel consumption of about 15 liters per 100 kilometers was unexpectedly low. The extremely shallow luggage space, on the other hand, was an annoyance, as it would not hold a typical suitcase.

In the same year, the journal *Das Auto, Motor und Sport* published a test report on the XK-E. After a thorough description of the car's unusual construction features, it was stated:

The interior decor is typically English in its sobriety and offers very little "interior safety." All in all, the car perhaps lacks some of the verve that Italian body constructors know how to give to cars of this type, but what with its long, low lines, it looks frightfully fast."

And the car proved to be very fast in terms of its statistics, reaching a top speed of just over 240 kph and accelerating from zero to 100 kph in just 6.8 seconds. The sports car's gentle nature surprised this journal's test driver too:

One would be inclined to forgive a car of this type if it were very loud and rough, but one cannot say this of the XK-E, for the motor runs very softly and smoothly. And the easy shifting also helps to make this very sporting car easy to drive on normal roads. The suspension is not soft, to be sure—in this respect the new Jaguar is more or less comparable with the Aston Martin GT, which likewise does not sacrifice its sporting character for the sake of a comfortable suspension."

The car's handling characteristics also earned unstinting praise, even though the test driver was less that 100% satisfied with the lack of feeling from the brakes:

"It reacts completely neutrally, in sharp curves it tends more toward under- than oversteering. In fast curves it can be controlled effortlessly, since its behavior can be controlled with the right dosages of the engine's enormous power. Nor does its directional stability at high speeds leave anything to be desired."

In August of 1969 the American magazine *Road & Track* tested a 4.2 liter coupe which already possessed emission control modifications to meet American requirements. The tester made clear at once what he did not like about the Series 2 car: "As fascinating as the XK-E was when it was introduced in 1961, it has since become old-fashioned inside and out. The interior, though it still smells nicely of leather and, with its millions of switches and gauges, reminds

Ruhmreiche Tradition

Renowned Tradition

No more famous tradition can probably be found than that which lies behind the new Jaguar 'E' Gran Turismo models. The Jaguar 'E' models were developed on the basis of the outstandingly successful records of the world-famous racing cars of the 'C' and 'D' Types. They were introduced as fast, elegant and luxuriously equipped touring cars and include all the characteristics that were created on the basis of a wealth of experience won in countless races.

The monocoque-style body was taken from previous Jaguar racing sportscar construction and consists of a non-flexing steel chassis with two subframes to hold the motor and rear axle unit, while the ingenious system of independent rear suspension represents a fully new concept, the result of long years of research and experimentation.

The world-famous 3.8 liter XK motor, Type 'S', with dual overhead camshafts and 3 carburetors, develops 268 HP and forms the power source of this impressive car, whose performance—with superfast acceleration and sensational top speed—works in harmony with the equally outstanding braking power and the high degree of driving safety. These attributes lend the car an extraordinarily high degree of safety.

A close examination of the specifications contained in this catalog shows that the 'Gran Turismo' models of the Jaguar 'E' Type are in all details—from the basic principles to the smallest details—the most advanced and modern sports car in the world.

Es kann wohl keine berühmtere Tradition gefunden werden als jene, welche den neuen Jaguar 'E' Gran Turismo Modellen zugrunde liegt. Die Jaguar 'E' Modelle wurden aus den, durch ihre überragenden Erfolgsrekorde weltberühmten Rennsportwagen der 'C' und 'D' Type entwickelt. Sie werden als schnelle, elegante und luxuriös ausgerüstete Touring-Type präsentiert und umfassen jene Charakteristiken, die aus den in unzähligen Fahrzeuge Rennsportveranstaltungen gewonnenen reichen Erfahrungen geschöpft wurden.

Die Karosserie im Monocoque-Stil wurde der bisherigen Jaguar-Rennsportkonstruktion entnommen und besteht aus einem verwindungssteifen Stahlgehäuse mit zwei Hilfsrahmen, zur Aufnahme der Motor- und Hinterachsaggregate, wohingegen das geniale System der unabhängigen hinteren Radaufhängung, eine vollkommen neue Konstruktionsart darstellt, der das Resultat langjähriger Forschungs- und Versuchsarbeit zugrunde liegt.

Der weltberühmte 3,8 Liter XK-Motor, Type 'S', mit doppelten obenliegenden Nockenwellen und 3 Vergasern, entwickelt 268 PS und bildet die Kraftquelle dieses aufsehenerregenden Wagens, dessen Leistung – mit ultraschneller Beschleunigung und sensationeller Höchstgeschwindigkeit – durch die überragende Bremskraft und den hohen Grad an Kontrollsicherheit, in ebenbürtigem Gleichklang steht. Diese Attribute verleihen dem Wagen ein außerordentlich hohes Maß an Sicherheit.

Eine genaue Durchsicht der in diesem Katalog enthaltenen Spezifikationen zeigt, daß die 'Gran Turismo' Modelle der Jaguar 'E' Type, in allen Einzelheiten – von den Grundprinzipien bis zu den kleinsten Details – die fortschrittlichsten und modernsten Sportwagen der Welt sind.

one of an airplane cockpit, causes the Jaguar to lack the roominess and ergonomic improvements of newer cars. Getting in and out is quite unpleasant, and the legroom is too small."

As far as driving impressions were concerned, the car had lost some of its charm for the test driver: "The handling characteristics of this newest XK-E are still typical of Jaguars, to be sure, but what with the emission control, a lot has been lost, and the air conditioning has also exacted its toll." But there was a lot that pleased the tester too: "The fully synchronized gearbox in use since 1965 is wonderful to shift, although it is not one of the quietest. The gearshift fits into the hand just right, and everything else is in just the right position, so that the XK-E ranks among the very few cars that one gets along well with right from the start."

In the end, the tester had the impression that the XK-E was still a fascinating car for many, but that the Jaguar firm had to be ready to deliver "something better" . . .

Test report published by the journal THE MOTOR in the Spring of 1961 shortly after the introduction of the model. Naturally the editorial staff of this great journal had been given the opportunity to test an example of the zero series in advance. In 15.1 seconds the car had reached 140 mph—225 kph.

The Motor Continental Road Test No. 10/61

Make: Jaguar **Type:** E-type

Makers: Jaguar Cars, Ltd., Coventry, England.

Test Data

World copyright reserved, no unauthorized reproduction in whole or in part.

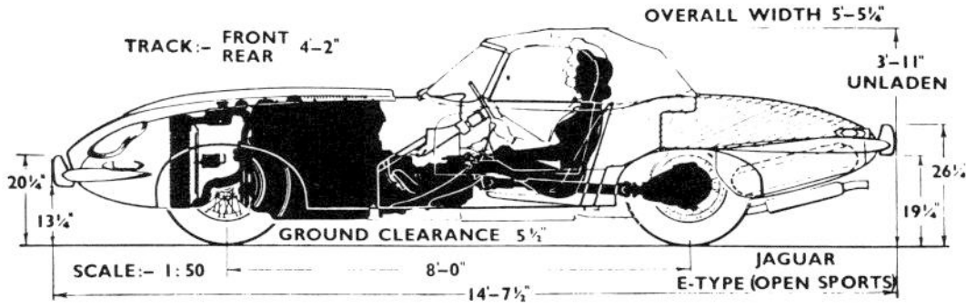
TRACK:- FRONT REAR 4-2"
OVERALL WIDTH 5'-5¼"
3'-11" UNLADEN
GROUND CLEARANCE 5½"
SCALE:- 1:50
8'-0"
14'-7½"
JAGUAR E-TYPE (OPEN SPORTS)

CONDITIONS: *Weather: Dry, warm, wind negligible. (Temperature 63°F. Barometer 30.5 in. Hg.). Surface: Dry tarmacadam. Fuel: Italian "Super" grade pump petrol (98-100 Octane Rating by Research Method).*

INSTRUMENTS

Speedometer at 30 m.p.h.	6% slow
Speedometer at 60 m.p.h.	1% fast
Speedometer at 90 m.p.h.	1% fast
Speedometer at 120 m.p.h.	accurate
Distance recorder	2½% slow

WEIGHT

Kerb weight, (unladen, but with oil, coolant and fuel for approx. 50 miles)	24 cwt.
Front/rear distribution of kerb weight	51/49
Weight laden as tested	28 cwt

MAXIMUM SPEEDS

Flying Quarter Mile

Mean of opposite runs	149.1 m.p.h.
Best one-way time equals	150.1 m.p.h.

"Maximile" speed. (Timed quarter mile after one mile accelerating from rest.)

Mean of opposite runs	136.4 m.p.h.
Best one-way time equals	136.4 m.p.h.

Speed in gears (at 5,500 r.p.m.)

Max. speed in 3rd gear	107 m.p.h.
Max. speed in 2nd gear	74 m.p.h.
Max. speed in 1st gear	40 m.p.h.

FUEL CONSUMPTION

(Direct top gear)

25 m.p.g. at constant 30 m.p.h. on level.
27 m.p.g. at constant 40 m.p.h. on level.
27½ m.p.g. at constant 50 m.p.h. on level.
27½ m.p.g. at constant 60 m.p.h. on level.
26½ m.p.g. at constant 70 m.p.h. on level.
24 m.p.g. at constant 80 m.p.h. on level.
22½ m.p.g. at constant 90 m.p.h. on level.
21 m.p.g. at constant 100 m.p.h. on level.
17½ m.p.g. at constant 110 m.p.h. on level.
14½ m.p.g. at constant 120 m.p.h. on level.
13½ m.p.g. at constant 130 m.p.h. on level.

Overall Fuel Consumption for 2,859 miles, 144.9 gallons, equals 19.7 m.p.g. (14.35 litres/100 km.).

Touring Fuel Consumption (m.p.g. at steady speed midway between 30 m.p.h. and maximum, less 5% allowance for acceleration) 21.3.

Fuel tank capacity (maker's figure). 14 gallons

STEERING

Turning circle between kerbs:

Left	39 ft.
Right	36½ ft.
Turns of steering wheel from lock to lock	2½

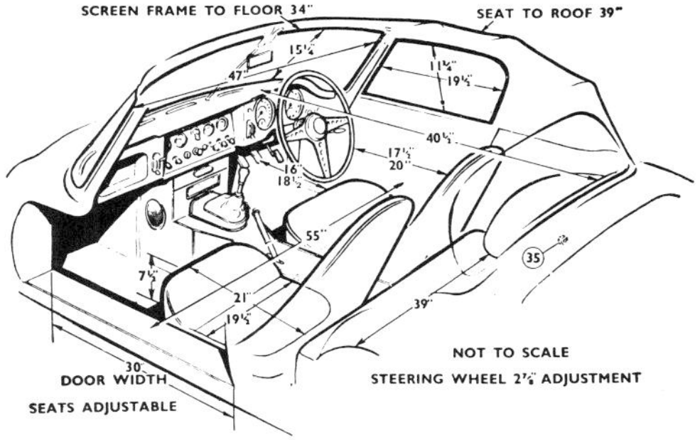
SCREEN FRAME TO FLOOR 34"
SEAT TO ROOF 39"
30"
DOOR WIDTH
SEATS ADJUSTABLE
NOT TO SCALE
STEERING WHEEL 2⅞" ADJUSTMENT

ACCELERATION TIMES from standstill

0-30 m.p.h.	2.6 sec.
0-40 m.p.h.	3.8 sec.
0-50 m.p.h.	5.6 sec.
0-60 m.p.h.	7.1 sec.
0-70 m.p.h.	8.7 sec.
0-80 m.p.h.	11.1 sec.
0-90 m.p.h.	13.4 sec.
0-100 m.p.h.	15.9 sec.
0-110 m.p.h.	19.9 sec.
0-120 m.p.h.	24.2 sec.
0-130 m.p.h.	30.5 sec.
0-140 m.p.h.	39.3 sec.
Standing quarter mile	15.0 sec.

ACCELERATION TIMES on Upper Ratios

	Top gear	3rd gear
10-30 m.p.h.	5.6 sec.	4.2 sec
20-40 m.p.h.	5.6 sec.	4.3 sec
30-50 m.p.h.	5.4 sec.	4.0 sec.
40-60 m.p.h.	5.4 sec.	4.0 sec
50-70 m.p.h.	5.3 sec.	3.9 sec
60-80 m.p.h	5.0 sec.	3.7 sec.
70-90 m.p.h.	5.2 sec.	4.2 sec.
80-100 m.p.h.	5.7 sec.	4.8 sec.
90-110 m.p.h.	6.6 sec.	6.5 sec
100-120 m.p.h.	7.7 sec.	—
110-130 m.p.h.	10.4 sec.	—
120-140 m.p.h.	15.1 sec.	—

BRAKES from 30 m.p.h.

1.00 g retardation (equivalent to 30 ft. stopping distance) with 115 lb. pedal pressure.
0.96 g retardation (equivalent to 31 ft. stopping distance) with 100 lb. pedal pressure.
0.79 g retardation (equivalent to 38 ft. stopping distance) with 75 lb. pedal pressure.
0.49 g retardation (equivalent to 61 ft. stopping distance) with 50 lb. pedal pressure.
0.22 g retardation (equivalent to 136 ft. stopping distance) with 25 lb. pedal pressure.

HILL CLIMBING at sustained steady speeds

Max. gradient on top gear	1 in 5 (Tapley 440 lb./ton)
Max. gradient on 3rd gear	1 in 3.7 (Tapley 585 lb./ton)
Max. gradient on 2nd gear	1 in 2.4 (Tapley 860 lb./ton)

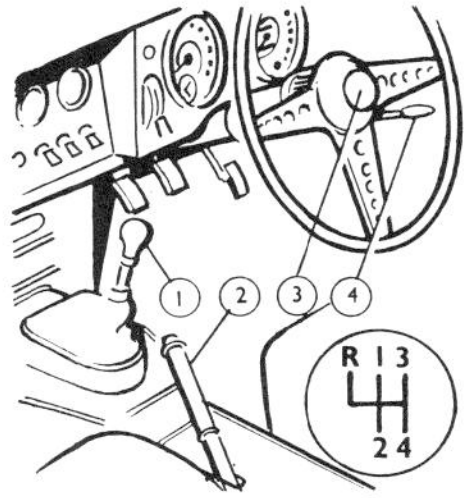
R 1 3
2 4

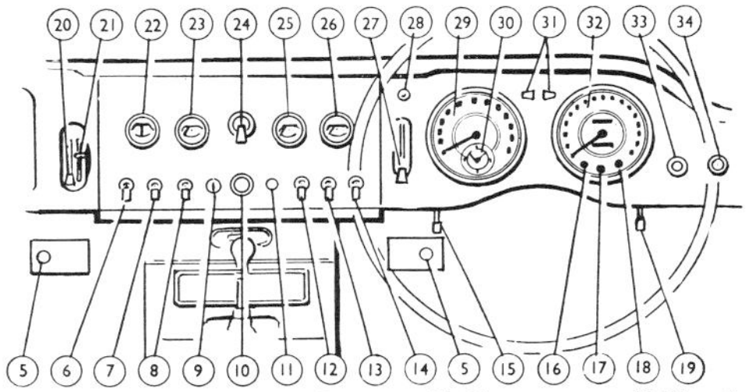

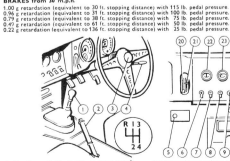

1, Gear lever. 2, Handbrake. 3, Horn button. 4, Direction indicator and headlamp flasher control. 5, Vent flaps. 6, Interior lights switch. 7, Bright-Dim panel light switch. 8, 2-speed heater fan control. 9. Ignition switch. 10, Cigar lighter 11, Starter 12, Map light switch. 13, 2-speed windscreen wipers control. 14, Electric screen washer control. 15, Clock adjuster. 16, Ignition warning light. 17, Fuel warning light. 18, Headlamp warning light. 19, Trip reset 20, Fresh air control 21, Heater control. 22, Ammeter 23, Fuel gauge. 24, Lights switch 25, Oil pressure gauge 26, Water thermometer 27, Choke. 28, Choke warning light. 29, Rev counter. 30, Clock. 31. Direction indicator warning lights. 32, Speedometer. 33, Handbrake and hydraulic fluid level warning light. 34, Dip switch. 35, Boot lid control (see middle drawing).

In fact, the 1971 XK-E was strongly upgraded once again, thanks to the wonderful new 12-cylinder motor. As early as May, *Ams* had the opportunity of testing the new model:

Whoever approaches the Jaguar prejudiced by Italian 12 cylinder motors, is in for a surprise: The British V-12 does not growl or bark, as its sporting colleagues from the south do so effectively. In fact, it is not at all sporting, but wins admiration by its paradoxical features, such as its soundless way of inhaling and exhaling, or the absolute lack of mechanical sounds. The Jaguar V-12, running more smoothly than a V-8, is quietly outstanding."

This splendid 12-cylinder motor with its 5.3-liter displacement provided fascinating driving experiences: "The soft humming that the starter awakens has a downright disappointing effect on the fan of mighty 12-cylinder engines. The power that he unleashes by stepping on the gas hits him all the more unexpectedly. Without the slightest acoustic expression, the V-12 of the honorable XK-E seems to want to achieve weightlessness. The long-nosed coupe accelerates in any gear, at any engine speed and, if you want, so strongly that the road soon seems too narrow, especially if the road in English."

It was not so much the absolute performance figures of the V-12, which were only marginally over those of the six-cylinder, that were so amazing as the heightened elasticity of the light-metal motor. From 800 rpm on up, one could accelerate powerfully, without bucking, and even at 6500 rpm the motor still behaved properly. But the new motor was not all that upgraded the XK-E:

"It is not only the motor that has changed this classic among sports cars so positively, but rather a whole series of detail changes. The car has gained noticeably in driving stability from the considerable stiffening of the tube frame, which stretches forward from the windshield and holds the motor and front suspension. Its road-handling profits from a wider track and considerably wider wheels and tires, its braking from a modified front suspension with anti-dive geometry."

Improved rack-and-pinion power steering also contributed to making this fast car easy and pleasant to drive.

Despite its relatively old age, the XK-E still ranked among the extraordinarily impressive cars to be seen on the road:

"We know the Jaguar XK-E too long to be confused by it, but it is still not without its charm today. Getting in over the high thresholds is somewhat difficult, and the seating area is narrow and warm from the heated drive tunnel, but the view over the endless engine hood is as impressive as ever, and gives one the feeling of sitting at the very end of the car." And further:

"Jaguar is absolutely right to assume that the 12-cylinder will get a warm welcome in America, because quiet power is appreciated there just as much as an image-building V-12. But the new XK-E presents itself in a form that, even in Europe, could make some old-timers stop and think. Such a decision will not be made any easier by the price, as that of the 5.3-liter V-12 is only about 2000 Marks higher than that of the still-produced 4.2!"

Series XK-E roadster of the 1969/70
model year—a timelessly elegant dream
car!

Model	XK-E 3.8	XK-E 4.2 Series 1	XK-E 4.2 Series 2	XK-E 5.3
Years Built	3/1961-10/1964	10/1964-9/1968	10/1968-9/1970	Roadster: 10/1970-2/1975 2 + 2: 4/1971-9/1973
Cylinders	6 in-line	6 in-line	6 in-line	V-12
Bore x stroke mm	87 x 106	92.07 x 106	92.07 x 106	90 x 70
Displacement cc	3781	4235	4235	5343
Compression	9 : 1 (8 : 1)	9 : 1 (8 : 1)	9 : 1 (8 : 1)	9 : 1
HP at rpm	268 at 5500	268 at 5400	268 at 5400	272 at 5850
Maximum torque at rpm	35.9 mkg at 4000	39 mkg at 4000	39 mkg at 4000	48.25 mkg at 3800
Carburetors	3 SU Type H D.8	3 SU Type H D.8	3 SU Type H D.8	4 Zenith 175 CDSE
Gearbox	4-speed, 2-4 synchronized	4-speed, fully synchronized	4-speed, fully synchronized	4-speed, fully synchronized
Wheelbase mm	2438	2438 2 + 2: 2670	2438 2 + 2: 2670	2670
Front/rear track mm	1270/1270	1270/1270	1270/1270	1387/1346
Length x width x height mm	4454 x 1657 x 1222	4454 x 1657 x 1222 2 + 2: 4780 x 1657 x 1270	4458 x 1657 x 1222 2 + 2: 4784 x 1657 x 1222	4684 x 1678 x 1270
Dry weight kg	1123	1275 2 + 2: 1417	1275 2 + 2: 1417	1558
Top speed kph	ca. 240	ca. 240 2 + 2: ca. 220	ca. 240 2 + 2: ca. 220	ca. 235 2 + 2: ca. 230
Acceleration 0-100 kph	ca. 7.2 sec. ca. 16 2. sec.	ca. 7 sec., 2 + 2: ca. 9 sec. ca. 17 sec. 2 + 2: ca. 19.2 sec.	ca. 7 sec., 2 + 2: ca. 9 sec. ca. 17 sec. 2 + 2: ca. 19.2 sec.	ca. 6.5 sec., 2 + 2: ca. 7 sec. ca. 15.5 sec. 2 + 2: ca. 16.5 sec.
Number made	Right-hand drive: Roadster: 942 Coupe: 1798 Left-hand drive: Roadster: 6885 Coupe: 5871	Right-hand drive: Roadster: 1182 Coupe: 1957 2 + 2: 1378 Left-hand drive: Roadster: 8366 Coupe: 5813 2 + 2: 4220	Right-hand drive: Roadster: 755 Coupe: 1070 2 + 2: 1040 Left-hand drive: Roadster: 7852 Coupe: 3785 2 + 2: 4286	Right-hand drive: Roadster: 1871 2 + 2: 2115 Left-hand drive: Roadster: 6119 2 + 2: 5182

Literature for the Jaguar Fan

Jaguar Automobile—Tradition und Technik eines Klassikers by Halwart Schrader. For the first time in German, this large-format volume offers a complete look at the history of the Jaguar firm and all its models produced to date. A wealth of fascinating, in part hitherto unpublished color and b/w photos makes this documentation an ideal gift for all those who love beautiful cars. In slipcase. 340 pp, 60 color and 300 b/w photos, 40 drawings, German text.

Jaguar—Geschichte—Technik, Sport by B. Viart and M. Cognet. In this volume the Jaguar sports cars (SS 100, XK 120 to 150, XK-E, XJS) are presented in words and pictures with all details. An impressive book for connoisseurs and fans. 440 pp, 460 photos, including 58 in color, German text.

Jaguar—The definitive history of a great British car by Andrew Whyte, with a foreword by Sir William Lyons. Exact descriptions and production statistics for every model to 1980, plus prototypes from prewar days and postwar competition cars are treated. 248 pp, 150 photos, English text.

Jaguar Sports Cars by Paul Skilleter. A lavishly produced photo volume portraying the development of all SS and Jaguar sports cars, with all technical data, racing results and information. 360 pp, 440 photos, English text.

Jaguar: The Complete Illustrated History by Philip Porter. An inclusive biography of the marque with all touring and sports cars into the Eighties. 160 pp, 330 b/w photos, 16 color pages, English text.

Jaguar—Great Marques by Chris Harvey with a foreword by Stirling Moss. After three volumes on Ferrari, Mercedes and Porsche, this beautiful picture volume has appeared, covering the Jaguar marque. 80 pp, 85 photos, 79 of them in color, English text.

Illustrated Jaguar Buyer's Guide by J. Hoehn. A guidebook for all collectors and fans of this marque. 156 pp, 150 photos, English text.

Jaguar Collector's Guide by Paul Skilleter. Every volume has 128 pp, ca. 150 photos, English text.

The Jaguar XK-E

Jaguar by Lord Montagu. This outstanding book on the marque, with much information on the firm and the cars, is now in its fifth fully reworked edition. 288 pages, 175 b/w photos and 16 color pages, English text.

Jaguar Cars by R. M. Clarke. In the Brooklands Series a number of volumes on the Jaguar marque have appeared. These reprints from contemporary publications offer an inclusive and thoroughgoing look at the history and technology of these models. Each volume in A4 format, ca. 100 pp, English text: **Jaguar XK-E 1961-1966, Jaguar XK-E 1966-1971.**

Brooklands Road & Track are reprints from this American magazine of road tests and technical data on a certain marque or production run. Each volume in A4 format, 92 pp, many photos, English text: **Road & Track on Jaguar 1961-68, Road & Track on Jaguar 1968-74.**

XK-E: End of an Era by Chris Harvey. This is one of the best historical and technical books on the Jaguar XK-E. Along with technical data, practical tips for restoration are offered. 236 pp, 125 b/w photos, 16 color pages, English text.

Jaguar E-Type by Denis Jenkinson. This volume of the Auto Histories Series treats the 3.8 and 4.2 6-cylinder and 5.3-liter V-12. 136 pp, 80 b/w and 12 color photos, English text.

E-Type: 3.8, 4.2 & 5.3 Litre, Jaguar Super Profiles. In this series from England, the authors give a detailed look at the history of an individual collector car. Reprints from contemporary journals, original works publications, addresses of clubs and workshops round off the picture. 56 pp, 20 color and 100 b/w photos, English text.

Jaguar E-Type—Operating, Maintenance and Service Handbook. Reprinted in English. A5 format, 77 pp, WK 1902, English text.

Jaguar E-Type 3.8 Spare Parts Catalogue. Reprint of the spare parts list. J30, A4 format, 334 pp, many photos, English text.

Jaguar E-Type 3.8 & 4.2, 1961-1972. Haynes Repair Guide No. 140, English text.

Jaguar E-Type 3.8 & 4.2, 1961-1972. Autobooks Repair Guide No. 758, English text.

Jaguar E-Type 3.8/4.2 Liter. Workshop handbook. BL E123/8/E123B/3.

Jaguar E-Type Series 3 Version 74. Spare parts list. RTC 9014.

Jaguar E Complete Official. This handbook by Bentley contains in one volume: Workshop handbook, driver's handbook and special tuning instructions for all 6-cylinder Jaguar E models. 412 pp, A4 format, 800 photos, drawings and diagrams, English text.

THE SCHIFFER AUTOMOTIVE SERIES

●●●●●●●●●●●●●●●●●●●●

The **Schiffer Automotive Series** features specific models and automobile manufacturers in detailed discussions and pictorial format. Each volume presents a different history of the models chronologically to show their development. Color and black-and-white photographs demonstrate the production, testing, and road use of each automobile. Technical information, contemporary advertisements, cut-away views, and detailed charts of parts and statistics supply important information for owners, restorers, toy collectors, and model buuilders. Each volume contains a list of specialized collector clubs worldwide for the benefit of all.

●●●●●●●●●●●●●●●●●●●●

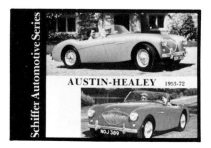

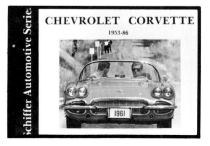